In A Perfect World…
My Daily Battle With Cancer

By Ginger McConnell

Copyright © 2008 Ginger McConnell

All rights reserved. No part of this book may be used or reproduced in any manner whatsoever without the written permission of the publisher.

ISBN: 978-0-615-24769-4

This book is dedicated to my "Little Man"
You are the light of my life

I also dedicate this book to my family – without you, this journey would have been impossible. Your love and support still carries me through my life daily….I love you!

I guess I need to explain a little bit about this book and its contents…

The words in italics - I wrote in my journal almost daily during my treatments. It was a way to get everything off of my chest without having to burden everyone around me – I could always tell my journal that I was scared or feeling bad and it wouldn't feel sorry for me!!

The entries with dates – I wasn't the only one who wrote in a journal during my treatments. My mom also wrote down everything that was happening, not only to me but my dad as well. My dad injured his knee and went through stuff just like I did, so I suspect my mom wrote in her journal to keep her wits about her!!

And the rest – The rest of the book is me writing my feelings looking back over my experience. I hope that these insights to my thoughts and feelings will help anyone – patient or caregiver – who is going through cancer.

I sincerely hope that this book will help you during your journey. I believe with all of my heart that I was diagnosed with cancer for a reason, and that God has plans for me and my story. That's why I'm here – and that's why I wrote this down for you.

The Calm Before The Storm...

Before cancer, the part of our lives that Tom and I affectionately call B.C., my life was the same as everyone else's – stressful, but good. In the year before being diagnosed, I had accomplished some great things. In May of 2000, I had graduated from Marietta College with a bachelor's degree in business management. Marietta College was a private college in my hometown that I had always dreamed of going to. It was such a proud day for me, along with my family, when I walked across that stage. I had also gotten a wonderful job with an insurance company, which took Tom and I to Zanesville, Ohio, which was about 1 hour away from our family. The job turned out to be something less than I expected, and I turned in my two-week notice right before my wedding.

During graduation, a new job, and moving to a new city, my mom and I were planning the wedding of my dreams. On August 19, 2000, Tom and I were married at The Wilds, in Cumberland, Ohio. The Wilds is an endangered species preserve where Tom had worked since 1994. It has an amazing hill that overlooks the preserve's acres of land. You can stand there and see giraffes, rhinos, and camels by just turning your head. One night, Tom took me on a trip to see the stars at The Wilds. Looking out over the lakes, I commented to Tom that this would be a beautiful place to have a wedding. "Okay, let's do it." At the time, I thought that Tom was just saying that to please me, so I didn't give it much more thought.

One day in October 1999, I was stressed out from my senior year of college. The leaves were turning, and I really wanted to get away from everything. I "persuaded" Tom earlier in the week to take me for a drive to look at the fall foliage. He agreed, and on Saturday morning, we headed out. He mentioned that we should drive up towards The Wilds because he was sure that the view was beautiful up there. I agreed, and we headed north. It had been raining the night before and the day was overcast, but I looked forward to relaxing.

When we arrived at the preserve, we drove to the top of the hill and talked a few minutes with some of his co-workers. I had noticed that Tom was carrying his binoculars, but didn't think too much about it. I thought that he might be looking for an animal while we were there.

We walked up to the top of the hill where the wind harp is located. I love this creation – when the wind blows through the piano string that is stretched along the top of the structure, it produces a humming. It's absolutely beautiful. We stood there for a few minutes, looking out over the landscape.

Tom then turned my attention to the field off to the side of the pasture. "Do you see anything over there?" he asked me. I looked, but it just looked like a field to me. "No, why, what do you see?" He had been looking through his binoculars at this field for a few minutes now. "Here, look through these and tell me if you see anything." He handed me the binoculars, and I looked again, still seeing nothing. "Look right at that group of bushes" he told me, moving behind me and pointing in the direction that he wanted me to look. I still could see nothing. I felt

Tom reach under my arm to help point me in the direction that he wanted me to look. By now, I was intently looking at this field, but could still see nothing. "Well, if it hadn't rained last night, you would see that it says *Will you marry me* on the hill." I looked down and Tom was holding a diamond ring in front of me. I turned around and looked at Tom's smile. He went on, "I'll get down on one knee if you want me to, but it's awful wet up here." I laughed and kissed him. "Yes!" I said!!

Tom explained that the night before, he had stayed after work and stomped down the grass in the field across from the preserve, kind of like making crop circles. When he came back to the site, he couldn't see the words very well and had gone to a small grocery store a few miles away and purchased flour. He went over his wording with the flour, to make it stand out. When he had left that night, he could see the letters perfectly. But the rain that night washed away all of the flour, making it hard to see. That's what he had been looking for in the binoculars!! He was so disappointed that his plan had failed. But I told him that it was the most romantic proposal that I had ever heard of. It was perfect just the way it was. (The following spring, the grass where the flour had been was greener than the other, and if you looked hard enough, the words "Will you marry me" were still there.)

The Wilds had always been a special place to Tom and I, and Tom asked permission to get married on the point that overlooked the pasture. The management gave us permission, and it was set. It took a lot of planning, but on Saturday, August 19, 2000, Tom and I were standing in front of 311 guests on the point at The Wilds. The day was perfect, along with the view. We had asked my pastor to perform the ceremony, which made it extra special. I couldn't have asked for anything more beautiful, or romantic.

Well, there was one little thing. That night, the temperature dropped to a record low of 50 degrees. Keep in mind that the point where our reception was held was on the second highest point in the state of Ohio, and it was definitely windy. The wind, along with the chilly temperature, made the night a little chilly. Okay, a lot chilly. A lot of the guests didn't hang around as long as we had hoped they would, but we could understand why they left. My dress was short sleeve and basically had no back, so I wore Tom's tux jacket around most of the night. Let's just say that it could have been a little warmer.

Tom and I left the next day for Las Vegas and the Grand Canyon. It was a great trip, and we had a great time. We didn't have to worry about being cold out there, I assure you!! When we returned from our honeymoon, work awaited us. The day after we returned home, we were packing up our belongings and moving back to Marietta. Zanesville was just an hour away from home, but it was too much for us. We found a great little apartment close to work and our family, and settled in. I got a job in a trust department at a local bank, and went to work two weeks after our move. Tom continued to work at The Wilds, and things seemed to be going as planned.

A couple of days after we moved in, I convinced Tom to let me have a cat. My Grandma's cat had had kittens, and there was one calico that I had my eyes on. We brought the little thing home with us and named her Samantha – Sam for short. She became our child – spoiled and all. We spent nights just playing with her. Sure, there were times that I wanted to throw her outside (like when she peed on my side of the bed, and my side only!!) but she always made me forget my anger by curling up on my lap and giving me that look – you know the one!!

After a few months in our apartment, the three of us were feeling crowded. We decided that we would look into getting our own place. We spent many weekends looking at doublewides and driving around the neighborhood looking at houses that were for sale. We always ended up coming home disappointed because what we really wanted was out of our price range. We didn't want to spend a lot of money on something that wasn't going to make us happy.

We started to toy around with the idea of building something. We had property next to Tom's parents, and we loved that area. After many hours of sketching, figuring, and finding the layout that we could both live with, we had our plan for our home. Actually, it was going to be a "temporary" home. We had a plan to build what would eventually be our garage – we would make it a very simple layout, and make it easy to convert to a garage once we saved enough money to build our permanent home beside the existing garage. Once we had the numbers in place, we realized that we would only be paying $16 more a month for this garage, which would be ours to keep, than what we were paying for rent on our apartment. We were both so excited – our dreams were starting to look attainable. It was early in the year, but 2001 was looking like it was going to be a great year; busy, but great.

I had always been active, playing as much softball as possible. It was a sport that I was good at, and enjoyed more than anything. I especially liked playing in the co-ed leagues. I enjoyed being able to compete with the guys. I remember when I was a little girl, I played little league with the boys. There was one specific time that I remember stepping up to the plate and the other teams coach yelled to the outfielders "Come in!! Move in, can't you see that it's a girl up to bat?!?" I made sure to give that coach a big smile as I rounded third base after I smacked a pitch over the left-fielders head.

In the spring, I decided to sign up for a co-ed softball league. I had been nursing a sore left knee, but that didn't stop me. I would play softball if my right arm were broken. We had a good team, but most of all, we had a good time. Tom had signed up to play, which was a stretch for him. He hated softball, but had decided to play so he could spend time with me – he knew that I loved the game.

After a few games, my knee started to really bother me. It hurt me when I ran to first base, which was not something that I wanted to deal with. I had noticed that there was a slight swelling above my knee - I must have hit it on something, explaining the pain I had been feeling. But as the pain continued, even with Tylenol, I decided I would go to a doctor to get it checked out. I hated to take any medicine, so if I could figure out what was wrong, I could fix it and avoid living the rest of my life on Tylenol and painkillers.

I went to a local quick care, and they took x-rays to see if they could detect anything. The doctor came in and explained that he thought I had arthritis in my knee. At 23, this was hard for me to believe, but I didn't have a reason not to trust what the doctor was saying. He told me to take more Tylenol and give it 10 days. If it still hurt after the 10 days, then I should call my family doctor and see him about the pain.

After 10 days of Tylenol and limping, I called my family doctor. I had to get this fixed, I couldn't stand not being able to play ball without pain. I had to wait about a week for the next appointment, but I got in. The doctor took one look at my x-ray, and agreed with the first doctor. He said that it was most likely arthritis, but that he would have to refer me to another doctor to take care of it. He figured that I would have to have arthroscopic surgery to remove the arthritis, and this doctor specialized in that surgery. The nurse scheduled an appointment with a local orthopedic doctor, and handed me my x-rays to take with me to the appointment.

I asked my doctor a very important question, one that I had been worrying about for a long time, "Can I still play softball? I have a game on Sunday."

He just smiled, "Do whatever you can tolerate." That's all I had to hear, and I walked out the door smiling.

Let the Tests Begin...

At my appointment with my orthopedic doctor, he looked at the x-rays and pressed on my leg, just like the others had done. He advised me that he wanted to get an MRI done on my knee before we decided on surgery. This would allow him to see what was really going on. He didn't give me any reason to worry, just had his nurse schedule the procedure for me, and said that I would come back to see him when he hears from the results – I was to tell them to send the results to him.

I had never had an MRI done, so my Grandma went with me, sort of to hold my hand. I was called back and went through one of the loudest procedures that I had ever part of. It took forever, and I had to stay perfectly still for the entire procedure – I fell asleep.

When the procedure was over, the nurse was helping me down off the table. "I'm supposed to have these films sent to my doctor, how do I do that?"

She looked at me shyly, "The technician is on the phone with him right now. We'll take care of it. Just go ahead out to the waiting room, and we'll be out to get you once we have the films."

I thought that it was kind of strange that the technician would call my doctor so soon after the procedure, but I went ahead out and sat with my Grandma. I explained that we needed to wait on the films, and we sat there reading magazines. The whole time, there was a suspension building up – what was going on, and why was this taking so long?

The nurse finally came out and handed me the films. "You are to call your doctor in his office tomorrow. He wants to talk to you about the test."

"Okay, I'll do that. Did they see anything?"

Well, she couldn't give me an answer, and I now can understand why.

I went back to work that afternoon, feeling more confused than before. If it was just arthritis, what took so long with the films? I decided that I would call and talk to my doctor today. I couldn't wait until the next day to find out what was going on.

I called the office and asked for the doctor. The nurse informed me that he was out of the office this afternoon, but would be back tomorrow. Was there something that she could help me with? I explained who I was, and what I was calling for. Surprisingly, she recognized my name and knew what was going on with my films.

"They found a lesion on your bone. The doctor will need to talk to you about what it is, and what we need to do now. Call him back tomorrow morning, and he can tell you more." There was a soft tone to her voice, and I detected a hint of sorrow or pity in her words.

"What is a lesion? What does that mean?" My mind was racing, I had no idea what was going on.

"We can't say for sure. You'll have to talk to the doctor. He'll be able to answer your questions."

As I hung up, a sick feeling started in my stomach.

Tuesday June 19, 2001
MRI M.M.H.
Dr. and the radiologist determined a lesion on the femur

I really had no idea what was going on. My idea of a lesion was a cut on the skin. This was strange, and the fact that I didn't know what the heck a "lesion" was really scared me. I had no idea what to think, and I can tell you that my mind was racing. I was told that I should call to talk to my doctor the next day. The next day I called from my office. That day, my office mate was out of the office and I was alone with all of my questions.

June 20, 2001
The doctor talked to Ginger more in length. At that time it was determined she has a tumor in the femur of her leg, and she will be sent to Columbus to a Dr. W.

I remember sitting at my desk and hearing the doctor say the word "tumor." So many things flashed through my mind when I heard that word. I was totally in shock. I really don't remember any of the other things that the doctor said during that conversation. I hung up the phone and looked around my empty office. What now? What do I do?

Tumors are always cancer, what if I had cancer? I don't want cancer – I'm too young to have cancer. Who ever heard of a tumor in the knee?

I needed someone to talk to. I walked out to Gwynne's desk, and stood there, wiping the tears away from my eyes. She looked at me and gasped, "What's wrong?" she asked. I explained that I just talked to my doctor. I remember saying "He said I have a tumor." I was sobbing and couldn't make myself stop. She asked me if I wanted to go back to my office and talk – all I could do was nod. She followed me back to my office and let me compose myself. I then explained to her what the doctor had told me. "You know, tumor doesn't always mean cancer." The statement didn't make me feel any better, but I nodded and agreed with her. "Yeah, I know."

6/21/01
Ginger talked to the doctor and he arranged a chest x-ray and a bone scan at MMH for Friday the 22nd. We also talked to him and he said Dr. W. is an Orthopedic Oncologist or a bone tumor specialist. She should get in first of the week.

The doctor had made this appointment sound like it was a life-or-death situation. I didn't realize how right he was. I had no idea why I needed tests ran before I went, especially a chest x-ray – the tumor was in my knee, not my chest. The bone scan required a shot of radioactive material – I hate needles, and the thought of radioactive liquid being injected into my veins didn't thrill me at all. As I lay there during the bone scan, I could see my body on the screen of the machine. The mass in my knee glowed a bright orange. I kept repeating over and over in my head – "it's not cancer, I'm going to be okay." I thought that if I kept repeating it, it would come true. I left the hospital with a band-aid on my arm and a knot in my stomach. I had no idea what to think, and I didn't want to think about anything.

6/22/01

Chest x-ray and bone scan were clear other than the knee

Looking back, I know that this was good news. No one explained the significance of these tests, but they just said that it was good.

6/25/01

Arranged an appointment with the orthopedic doctor at 4:30 on Tuesday to be worked in at Columbus.

Dr. W. was going to be out of town, so this was the only time that I could get in. It wasn't actually an appointment, but Dr. W. told me to come up anyway. He would fit me in.

6/26/01

Dr. Larry W. MD did a biopsy on Gingers knee and told us she has a giant cell tumor in her femur and the mass has grown into her knee, she will have extensive surgery after the biopsy come back which will consist of plastic and rods. She can't walk on her leg until after surgery because she could break her fragile bones. We should know Friday on the biopsy.

Sitting in Dr. W.'s waiting room, I was exposed to a whole different world. Sitting around me were folks with crutches and scars, which wasn't that different. But then a little boy walked in the door with a mask on. This was the first time I had ever seen anyone out in public with a mask on, let alone a little boy. I watched him and his family walk up to the desk to sign in and notices that one leg was much skinnier than the other. As I looked closer, I noticed that he had a long scar from the top of his leg to the middle of his shin. Wow, I thought, that was some surgery. My heart really went out to this boy, but he seemed so happy and content. It didn't bother him a bit that his leg was different. The nurse came out and ushered him and his family back into a room. I noticed that they all were smiling as they walked back through the door.

I sat in that waiting room with my mom, dad, and Tom until we were the last ones there. We waited there for four hours. We had seen the little boy and his family walk out, still smiling. We had seen patients with many different conditions go in and out of the office. Finally, the nurse come out and called my name. She explained that she had let the boy and his family go into the room first because the little boy had just finished a round of chemotherapy. His blood levels made him very susceptible to germs, and getting sick was very dangerous for him.

When Dr. W. came into the room, I must admit, he wasn't what I pictured. Actually, I'm not sure what I expected at all. A student doctor, who seemed scared as he followed the doctor in, accompanied him. He took the x-rays that we had brought from Marietta and put them up on the lighted screen. He showed us where the tumor was in my femur, and explained that he would have to do a biopsy to see what type of tumor it was. He did say that he thought it was a giant cell tumor, and that it would involve surgery to be removed. He explained how it started inside of the bone and made the bone very brittle. As he talked, a lump was forming in my stomach. Dr. W. could see what I was thinking, and he looked at me with a smile. "Giant cell tumors are non-cancerous 90% of the time." And there it was, the knot in my stomach vanished. I laughed with relief.

He explained that to be sure, he needed to take the biopsy. He asked me to lie down on the table in the room. He decided that he would let his intern do the biopsy – this was a decision that made me a little nervous. I didn't really want the doctor to poke at me, let alone someone who had never done this kind of thing before. I decided to put my faith in the hands of this young student, and took a deep breath. This was the only way to know that what Dr. W. had said about the giant cell tumor was true.

I will say that the biopsy was the most disgusting and painful thing that I had to endure during my entire treatment. And, believe me, I went through a lot of stuff. First thing that they did was numb my leg – a true blessing. I can't imagine what this ordeal would have been like without the blessing of that little shot. I didn't know what to expect from this procedure, so everything was a surprise. I thought that they would use a needle to take a sample – instead, it was a gizmo the width of a McDonald's straw that was jabbed into my leg. To this day, I can't use a straw without remembering that experience. I was thinking that it would probably feel like a shot – instead, it was more of a probing. They attempted to take a sample three times, and only one try, the first, gave them a usable sample. Every time they tried to get another sample, they would twist and turn the probe around in my leg. The feeling made my stomach queasy. During the procedure, Dr. W. commented that there was a lot of blood, which was common for a giant cell tumor. Even though I was in complete agony, this phrase comforted me. I could feel every time they went in to get another sample, every time the instrument went deep into my leg. It wasn't a sharp pain; it was more of a dull type of feeling. As the doctor explained, the probe was going through my bone, into where the tumor was located. I remember trying to look and see what they were doing. I picked up my head and Tom, who was sitting behind me, instinctively took my face in his hands. He looked me right in the eyes with a sincere calmness, "Look right here," he said, and gave me a smile. His touch made me feel safe.

After the procedure was over, I tried to sit up. That was definitely a short-lived idea. I started to feel light-headed, and turned pale white. "Lay back down, honey. Take your time." The nurse was so nice and caring. She got me a washcloth and a glass of water. They explained that the student's first attempt was the only successful sample that they got, but it was good enough to use.

Dr. W. was going to be out of town the following week, but he promised that he would call me with the results of the test. He told me not to walk on my leg because the tumor had eaten at my bone, and made it brittle. The worst thing that could happen, he explained, was the bone breaking. I promised that I would get crutches as soon as I got home.

Tom helped me hop to the car, and we settled in for a two-hour drive home. As the four of us left that office, we felt like a load of bricks were lifted from our shoulders. We were all so relieved that we called all of our family from the cell phone on our way home. Dr. W. had explained that I would have to have a knee replacement surgery to remove the tumor and repair the weakened femur, but that there would be nothing more to it. I decided on the way home that I could handle a surgery. I was just content to hear that he didn't think it was cancer.

The News No One Expected…

<u>6/29/01</u>
<u>The surgeon called to tell us the tumor was 95% sure to be cancer. The final pathology report will be back Monday. She will need further testing, and the surgery will be more extensive.</u>

It was Friday afternoon, and Dr. W. had told me that he would call me today with news about the results. When I saw a number on the caller id that I didn't recognize, I guessed it was him. I answered the call with excitement – this is the news that I needed to get on with my life. When I answered the phone, I didn't expect the news that I was going to get.

Dr. W. explained that the test had shown that it was likely that my tumor was malignant. The shake in my voice led to more explanation – "It's 95% sure to be cancerous."

No matter what you think you would do, no matter how many different ways you imagine it, you will never know what your reaction to such a phrase would be. In an instant, I was transported to a different world. I had a feeling of complete helplessness. Dr. W. told me that the top hematologist at the James Cancer Center in Columbus, Ohio was looking at my sample. He said that this wasn't a definite thing, and that he would call me on Monday with the findings of the hematologist.

Now what? I was left with two days to think about this news. I was totally dazed. I don't even remember how Tom found out about the call. I don't remember telling my parents what Dr. W. had unloaded on me. I almost wished that Dr. W. would have waited until the news was certain before he called me. Now I was left to wait and see if the worst news of my life was true.

That Saturday, Tom and I went to the Independence Day fireworks at our county fairgrounds with a couple of our friends. I was on crutches, and remember that the only seats that were available were high on the grandstand. Tom followed close behind me as I navigated up the steps and to the seat. The conversation was light and fun for the other three, and it probably seemed like it was the same for me. Underneath the smile, I was a mess. I watched the fireworks and couldn't help but thinking that they might be the last that I would see.

I asked Tom to take me to the Wilds on Sunday afternoon. I wanted to get away from everyone and everything. He drove me to the top of the hill and we walked out the point together. I couldn't help but think that it was less than a year ago that we had stood in this very place and were married. It was the happiest day of my life. Now, I was relying on this place to relax me. Tom and I sat on the bench at the end of the point and looked out over the pasture. I thought that I would like to stay in the place forever. Maybe the world wouldn't find me here. Maybe I wouldn't have to face anything if I sat here for the rest of my life.

7/2/01
We received word from Dr. W. that Ginger's cancer is serious and is Osteogenic Sarcoma. She is going to have 2-3 months of

chemotherapy, then surgery and replace the knee with a steel knee, then another year of chemo. This can be a life threatening cancer. She will be going to Children's Hospital in Columbus. She'll have a long term I-V put in and more testing done. We should know tomorrow when we'll make our next trip to Columbus.

Tom was working midnights at his job, and was scheduled to go to work at 6:00 pm that night. Come 5:30 pm that night, we had not heard from Dr. W. Tom didn't want to leave for work.

"Go ahead and go. I will call you if he calls once you get there. Don't worry about me, I'll be okay."

It took about five more minutes of prodding, but Tom finally left for work. I sat there with Sam, watching Oprah. I finally had some time to relax by myself, and I sat there petting Sam. The phone broke into my peace. Dr. W. was on vacation, and was calling from his cell phone from wherever he was.

I honestly don't remember the details of the conversation. I do remember that I didn't cry – I was shaking, but there were no tears. I had to write down what he told me; phone numbers and tentative schedules of appointments. I do remember thanking him for calling me on his vacation – he sort of laughed and told me that it wasn't a problem.

I hung up the phone and sat there in shock. What just happened? I had no idea what I was feeling. I was basically numb. I knew that I needed to call other people, but I needed to set there and let it sink in. Sam came back up on the couch and sat on my lap – I think that she understood that something was wrong. She rubbed against my hand, sort of telling me that she loved me. It was this sign of affection that made the tears well up in my eyes. I finally let the seriousness of the news hit me – why me? I'll admit that it was one of the first things that I thought. I sat there, crying and sobbing, letting the emotions take over.

After a few minutes, I regained as much of my composure as I could, and dialed the phone to call Tom at work. What do I say? How do I break it to him that this is serious? Our friend, Josh, answered the phone.

"Josh, is Tom there?"

Josh knew what was going on, and tried to lighten the situation, which I did appreciate – it made me smile.

"Hey Gingee – I'll get him for you."

Just a few more minutes and I had to tell my husband that I had cancer. I was shaking again. He came to the phone.

"Hello?"

"Um, hey. The doctor called."

"And?"

"It's cancer, Tom."

"I'll be home right home."

I hung up the phone – there were the tears again. I couldn't stop them. They were uncontrollable. But there was another call I had to make.

"Dad – the doctor called. It's not good news."

I didn't have to explain anything in detail.

"Is Tom there?"

I explained that he was on his way home right now, and dad told me that they would be down in just minutes. I hung up the phone again, still feeling empty and numb.

But it didn't stop there – I dialed the phone again to my Aunt Linda. I just needed to talk to someone – I couldn't stand sitting there by myself. Aunt Linda answered the phone, and she knew that something was wrong the minute I said her name. I don't think I remember more than twice in my lifetime that I have ever known my Aunt to cry, but I knew that she had started to cry, too. I explained what Dr. W. had told me, and she, too, offered to come down to the apartment. I looked out the window and seen that mom and dad were just pulling in. I told

Aunt Linda that mom and dad were already here, and I would call her later.

Aunt Linda explained later that after she hung up the phone, she lost her composure. She said she was mad at the world and didn't understand why it had to be me. I am extremely close to my Aunt and there is no way that I could have told her my news face-to-face. It would have just broken my heart to see her reaction.

Mom and dad came through the door and immediately I saw their tears. My dad was at my side in an instant, and I buried my face in his chest. We were both sobbing, and we sat there together for a few minutes. My mom had sat down on the other side and I hugged her so tight that I could hardly breathe. We didn't have to say a word to each other – we all knew what was going through each other's mind.

I heard Tom pull in and shut off the car. My mom moved over to the chair and Tom walked right in and sat down beside me. He put his arms around me, and we sobbed together, too.

It was one of the few times that I seen Tom cry. I mean, tears – yes, but not like this. I wanted to hold him and tell him that it was going to be okay – I was going to be okay. But I knew that he just needed some time. I'm not sure how long we sat there together, crying and talking about what we couldn't believe.

We decided that the rest of the family had to be told, but wasn't sure how to do it. I decided that I needed to tell them in person. I wasn't sure how that was going to go, but I knew that it had to be done that way. I crutched out to mom and dad's car and the four of us started a long drive, and a long night.

I guess this is when I started to develop the strong attitude that I *tried* to carry through the entire treatment. I just felt that my family wouldn't cope with what was about to happen if I was moping around and crying all of the time – that wasn't my personality before treatment, and it definitely wasn't going to be my personality during treatment. Now I'm not saying that I was always strong, but only a few people seen my cry. I made sure of that. My family was so strong, but they had also already been torn apart by cancer, and I couldn't see letting that happen again.

No, my family was no stranger to cancer and the pain that it can cause. When I was four years old, my mom, Kandis Kay Moore, died of cancer. She was pregnant at the time, and so my family not only lost mom, but a baby boy as well. It was so unexpected – such a shock. This loss left my dad alone to raise me – and with the help of my Grandpa & Grandma Broome, Grandpa & Grandma Moore, and Aunt Linda, that's what they did.

I was only four when my mom died, so I don't remember the things that my family went through the days after. I do remember being at the funeral home and seeing my mom lying there. I had no idea what was going on. In fact, throughout my life, I carried just a few memories of my mom. But the one thing that was a constant in my mind when I thought of her - cancer always meant death to me. It's all that I had known. And I knew that, even though my dad had married four years later to a wonderful woman (who would eventually become my best friend), I still had a hole in my heart that would never fully heal.

And now here I was, facing cancer. And it was because of this history that we began with my mom, Kay's, parents – it just felt like I needed to tell them first. As we pulled in to see Grandpa Dean and Grandma Betty, I got really nervous. Everyone knew that I was expecting to hear from the doctor – what would they think when the saw us pull in? We got out of the car, and made our way to the porch, where the six of us sat.

I don't remember exactly how I said it. I know that it was a speech that I repeated many times that evening. The four of us went to every grandparents house, first Grandma & Grandpa Broome's, then Grandma & Grandpa Grosz's, on finally to Grandma Opal and Denny's. Each time, there was a different reaction. Every stop I explained what I thought the schedule was going to be and I didn't show that I was scared. I made myself be strong for my family.

Children's Hospital...

7/6/01

Ginger heard from Cindy at Children's Hospital and gave her an appointment for the following Thursday at 12:30. Children's Hospital # is 1-614-XXX-XXXX. Cindy at Children's said Ginger's bone scan that was done at MMH was fine and wouldn't have to be repeated. Ginger will have a Chest CT, physical and blood work done on Thursday and will meet with Dr. O. to talk about her chemotherapy at 1:30. Colleen the nurse at Dr. W.'s office and Angie have been really helpful.

When I heard that I couldn't get up to the hospital until the following Thursday, I was really confused. The had told me that the type of cancer that I had was a fast growing cancer, and that I would need to get things taken care of right away. So why wasn't I getting an appointment the next day? Why wasn't I already there? And why more tests? They already knew that I had cancer, what else did they need to know? I was so frustrated – I wanted to get things started. My idea was that the sooner I get started, the sooner I was done.

7/12/01

We went to Columbus, Outpatient department at Children's Hospital 555 South 18th St. to the radiology dept. across from the E.R., for the CT Chest scan at 12:30 then up to the 4th floor at 1:30 to meet Dr. O. a Hematologist. Instead of Dr. O., we saw Dr. E. He told us Ginger will have bloods tests, hearing test, kidney test, EKG and EEG of her heart done and possibly the other tests ran again before she has her port put in. After all the results are back she'll start the chemo. She'll meet a psychologist, dentist, personal nurse, etc before her stay in the hospital the first time.

Dr. "Reggie" was awesome. He was from Africa, so it took all four of us to understand what he was saying. I would concentrate for a few sentences, and then lose him and hope that Tom got what he was saying.

Dr. "Reggie" was concerned about me being in any pain, and I do mean any. He asked me at least five times if I was in any pain. I told him no each time, but he always responded with, "If you're in any pain, I can prescribe you some good drugs. You don't have to be in pain – you shouldn't be in pain." After he left the room, mom, dad, Tom & I laughed so hard, we forgot where we were for a minute. We joked that he sounded like a drug dealer who wanted to sell me some "good drugs." But we all felt comforted with the gesture of medicine; it made us see that he had my best interest at heart. As the time went on, I realized that there wasn't a person at Children's Hospital who didn't have my best interest at heart.

7/13/01
Received word from the hospital to be back there Monday at 8:00 for the kidney test and the audio test. Then on Tuesday AM Ginger will have the EEG and EKG done then the port put in surgically and the chemo started.

7/16/01

Had a Hem Renal test done, she was injected with radioactive material for 15 minutes, photos taken then 2 hours later, 2 ½, 3 and 3 ½ hours later blood was drawn, this test will be repeated every 2 months to watcher her kidneys. They can't use the port in her chest to do this because of the radioactivity.

The audio test Ginger had will be repeated every 6 weeks.

We return on Tuesday for an echo of Gingers heart and an EKG before they put in the port and start the chemo. She weighs 134#.

We spoke with Dr. Reginald "Reggie" before we left and found out that Gingers Chest CT came back clear. Since she is clear of cancer in her lungs that makes her eligible for protocol phase 1, she'll have two days of chemo at a time instead of five which we had originally thought. He went over the side effects and the drugs that she would be given and the dosages. She will have surgery in 11 weeks if everything goes well. Surgery is at 1:30 for the port.

7/17/01
Arrived at 10:00 for the heart echo and EKG. Registered in outpatient surgery at 11:00 for the port. The surgery was at 1:30, Ginger was in her room by 3:00. Repeated the bone scan at 7:30. We stayed at the Ronald McDonald House and Tom stayed in her room.

I don't know if I've mentioned it before this, but I HATE needles. This surgery was explained as a simple procedure, but I knew that needles were involved, so I was really scared by this. Plus, I had never been in the hospital before, let alone surgery. This was a first for me, in many ways. I was sitting in the waiting room with my family surrounding me. Everyone was putting on a really good face, but I assumed that everyone was nervous for me – they didn't know what to expect, either.

We were only allowed to have 2 visitors with me in the prep room, so Tom and dad came back with me. They wheeled me in a room and asked me to get into a bed. Beside me, there was a little boy who was getting surgery, too. His mother was sitting with him, and they were watching cartoons. The nurse came by to see if I needed anything, but I told her no. There we sat – my dad, Tom and myself – all of us smiling on the outside, but worried on the inside. I was told that I was not allowed to wear my contacts during surgery, so I was wearing my glasses.

The nurse came over and started to prepare me for surgery. She took my glasses, so now I couldn't see anything. She also asked me my favorite scent. The question threw me off – she explained that they had scents that they would rub onto my oxygen mask, so that I wouldn't have to smell the rubber. The boy next to me had picked bubble gum, and he let me sample the flavor. She had a list of about 8 different smells – it was like I was at an ice cream store!! I selected strawberry.

The doctor came in and asked if we had any questions about the surgery. We didn't, but he stayed with us for a few minutes. He seemed like a nice enough guy.

They finally came in to take me back to my room for surgery. I said my goodbyes to Tom and dad, holding back my tears so they wouldn't know that I was scared. They wheeled me down many halls and stopped outside of the surgery room. I looked around, but couldn't really see anything without my glasses. The hallway was dark and dreary, and was definitely depressing. My surgical nurse was standing at the bottom of my bed, and she explained that we were waiting for the room to finish being cleaned. She was so sweet, and I remember thinking it was too bad that I couldn't see her face – I would only have a blurry memory of her. After what seemed like eternity, and telling two of the surgery nurses my story of how I ended up where I was, they wheeled me into a cold, green room. In an instant, the whole surgery team appeared, scrambling around the room.

A man appeared at my side and informed me that he would be inserting the IV for my anesthesia. He took my left hand and lowered it below the table. After I looked at him with a worried face, he explained that by lowering the hand over the table, it made the veins pop up, and made his job easier. And, he said, made it easier on me. Well, he was a nice guy, but he missed the first time. I thought – great, what a great start to a great day. Another nurse took my other hand and rubbed my cheek. "Just take a few deep breaths; you won't have to worry about being cold any more. And, I promise, we'll take good care of you." Her kind words made me relaxed and I took two deep breaths. The last thing I remember is hearing her say, "Good night...."

I don't remember anything else until I woke up in my room on the Hematology floor. I remember everything being dim, and my dad saying "Hey kiddo." I started to sit up in the bed and a twang of pain shot up my right arm. Oh, yeah, my port. A thought entered my mind instantly: my right shoulder, my throwing arm – why did they put it in my throwing arm? It didn't occur to me at that time that I wouldn't be playing softball ever again, and that it didn't matter which side they put it in.

There was a sudden feeling of hunger, and I asked my dad for something to eat. I don't remember much of what I ate, but I do remember thinking that the food wasn't half bad for hospital food.

Chemo...

7/18/01

Did the second MRI at 2:30. We talked to Stacy her personal nurse. Her surgery will be at James Cancer Center the first week of October or (11 weeks from today the first day of chemo.) She will have blood drawn next week and the following week. The third week she'll be back in Columbus for a 4-6 day stay for her second round of chemo. This will be three weeks in a row. The chemo that Ginger is being given was chosen through a study comprised at St. Jude's and Johns Hopkins for a national study. Case manager Stacy & Amanda is the nurse practioner. Ginger will be released 48 hours from the time she is done with her first treatment. Gingers Rm # is 5311 and her phone # is 1-614-XXX-XXXX. Started hydration at 5:15. Gingers double port is flushed with heparin before and after use. Ginger was hydrated the second try and she started her first chemo at 10:00 pm and her last at 12:00 pm.

Let me tell you, there were so many numbers, dates, blood counts, etc. thrown at me and my family that first week, there was no way that I would have been able to remember them all. I felt so overwhelmed and so confused. It was like I was in a totally different world. I figured out in the next few months that I really was. I do know that it is a scary world, the world of cancer. And this world is different for everyone, and it's also the same.

I sit here in room 5311 at Children's Hospital – Columbus, Ohio. I have just finished getting my first dose of chemo. I have met so many people – their names are swarming around in my head. Actually, there are a lot of things that are floating around in there.

Since March of this year, I have known that there was something wrong with my knee - I just didn't know what. After x-rays and exams, doctors in Marietta thought I had arthritis and I would need surgery to scrape it away. Then, after an MRI, they discovered it was a tumor. After a lot of tests, needles, pokes, x-rays, etc., here I sit with osteogenic sarcoma. All I can see of the tumor is swelling above my left knee – it's so hard to imagine it's actually a threat to my life.

At first, I couldn't say the word "cancer". I was really too scared to mention the idea. To me, cancer has always meant death. Now, I am starting to see that it doesn't have to mean that at all. I do see that it's not just my disease; it's a disease that is my family's and friends. It means a lot of sacrifice and change for everyone involved. I'm not sure how often I can work, if I can be "normal." I'm even nervous about going out in public without my hair. But I realize that all of these worries and sacrifices aren't as big as the end result – getting better and continuing my life.

OK – enough with that stuff, on with day-to-day life. The stuff I am currently hooked up to makes me go to the bathroom, so every hour or so, I have to get all of my stuff together and wheel my way into the bathroom. And I have to pee in a "hat" then call the nurse's station and report the fact that I went to the restroom. They need to keep really strict records to make sure all the stuff they put in me actually comes out of me.

Everyone is really nice up here. They're used to having to deal with kids. I think I'm a welcome change. Tonight my nurse is Tiffany – she's really funny and Tom really likes her.

Yes, Tom. He is trying to sleep on a pull-out couch. He has really done great here. I know it has to be hard for him and he's putting on a great face for everyone. I am sad that I can't be a normal wife for him, at least, not yet. We had so many plans – house, children, etc. They will have to be put on hold for a while. Actually, the house plans are going on without us – there's a group of guys that will be building our house for us (more on that later!) Anyway, Tom is great, and will continue to be. I hope some day I can be as great for him. I love him so much.

Mom and dad came up Tuesday with us for my surgery (putting in my port – ouch!) They left tonight about 7 pm, so I'm sure they're tired. I know they are both worried, but they seemed more relaxed before they left. Dad tried so hard to act like things were okay, but I knew that he was nervous and worried. I think they will rest better tonight.

Well, I think that's all for now. Time for vitals, going to pee and then to sleep.

7/19/01

Ginger did well with her chemo she was a little queasy but no vomiting. They will give her a second day of chemo at 7:00 pm today. She vomited a few times during the night, she said the sick feeling comes on quick and leaves quick.

I will tell you that this first dose of chemotherapy was nothing like I thought it would be. The night before, I had sat there and watched the chemo being pumped into me. I had fully expected to feel the toxin burning inside of me. I thought that I would get violently ill the instant that the fluid hit my blood. I had sat there, just staring at it, as it dripped down the IV tube and into my port. It was red – funny, it put me in the mind of kool-aid. Boy, I wish.

As time went on, I did finally loose my appetite. And, there was finally vomiting. But it was nothing like I had imagined. I had always pictured a cancer patient always being sick and tired. I thought that I would be puking from day one, and then sleeping my way through the rest of treatment.

10:30 am
This is going to be a day of visitors, so I thought I would try to keep track of who I talk to.

The Chaplin came to talk. He seemed sort of surprised at my attitude and said I was a treat to talk to. He prayed with me before he left. He seemed like a really nice guy.

<u>7/20/01</u>
<u>Was resting and hydrating to ready herself to be released, she has to be able to keep solid food down first. She left the hospital at 10:00 pm and arrived home at 12:30 am.</u>

A Day I'll Never Forget...

<u>7/21/01</u>
<u>50 families got together and built Tom and Gingers apartment/Garage, we had our meals at Dave & Linda's. It was a great day.</u>

A great day – three little words that can't even begin to touch how immense this day was for us. Our future had seemingly been put on hold by my diagnosis, and then comes this miracle. My mom kept telling me what was being donated and by who, and it boggled my mind. I had always wondered how people would react to the news of my diagnosis, you know, "Oh, she's so young. How could this happen?", that kind of thing. Well, this was a reaction that I had not expected.

I came home from my first chemo to see my house framed and standing. People were walking around with tools and lumber, not really noticing how awesome of a sight this really was. I wasn't allowed to be close to the construction – too much dust and dirt for my to-be fragile immune system – so I had to stay in the car and put on a mask so I wouldn't breathe in the dust. Sitting in the front seat of our car, I was so overwhelmed with the site and the out-pouring of love, that I couldn't even cry. I didn't even know what to say. How do you thank 50+ people for making your dream come true?

<u>7/22/01</u>
<u>A work crew started to shingle the garage roof at 7:00, we were to have soup beans at Carol and Gary's for lunch. At 11:00 the</u>

scaffolding gave way and six men fell off the steep side of the garage. Roger had a dislocated knee and two fractures in his leg and ankle. Allen was transported but only had a sprained shoulder, ankle & hand. Roger had a closed reduction surgery at 6:00pm-8:00pm. He will go to Columbus to Grant hospital to see a doctor in a few days. Aaron, Mike, Matt & Garrett were also on the scaffolding when it collapsed. Ginger had a reasonable appetite for chicken noodle soup, toast & jello.

I wondered what was going on when Tom came home early from the building site. And then, all of the happiness from the previous day drained instantly away with this news. My dad was my rock, and he was hurt doing something that he wanted so badly to do for me. No words can explain how helpless and hopeless I felt in that moment. I wanted to go and see him, but hospitals were out of the question with my battered immune system. So, not only was I sick and scared myself, but I found myself in a situation that I couldn't do anything for my dad either.

7/23/01

Ginger was a little sick in the morning but had grilled cheese and cookies & cream ice cream later in the day. The doctor in Marietta decided to send Roger to Monongalia Hospital in Morgantown, WV for surgery. They sent Roger by squad at 8:30 pm; we arrived at 10:45 in Morgantown. He was taken to Ruby Memorial by mistake; they tried to admit him in room #637 which was O.B. We arrived at the right hospital at 11:15. Opal and I stayed at an Econo Lodge from 2:00 am-9:00am. Had an MRI at MMH.

7/24/01

The doctor decided to postpone surgery from 6-8 weeks to let the leg heal as much as possible. Had x-rays, therapy and leg blood pressure. He was discharged at 7:00 pm. Completed the roof on the garage.

7/25/01

We got Gingers handicapped placard. She was weak and had a passing out spell.

I don't think that the phrase "had a passing out spell" really describes the situation accurately. I wasn't scared – I didn't grasp what was going on at the time. But Tom, now that's another story. He knew exactly what was happening and he didn't know how it was going to end up. Poor guy, he had so much stress on him at the point, and this ended up being the straw that "broke" his back.

As I describe in my following journal entry, I was sleeping in the bed and Tom was on the couch. He thought that this would be better for me – more comfortable for me. He was right, but I still missed him beside me. I had to sleep alone while I was in the hospital. It was early in the morning, and I wasn't sleeping very much. I had to go to the bathroom, which meant about five minutes of preparation before I could actually get to the bathroom. I was so tired, but I knew that I should get going. I rounded up my crutches and started out of the bedroom. As I closed the door behind me, I started to feel fuzzy – there were dots around me. I sat down on the side of the tub and rested for a minute. The fuzziness went away, and I decided to head back to bed.

Using the crutches was hard for me at this time, because of the soreness in my right arm from my port surgery. I slowly plotted my way out of the bathroom and started into the bedroom. The fuzziness and spots began to appear again, only they came on faster than before. Suddenly, I started to loose sight and feeling woozy.

"Tom, I need you."

Tom was sound asleep in the living room, and didn't hear me – "What?"

"I need you in here!!"

My voice was fading in and out in my head, and then the stars took over, and my mind starting fading as well. Then, black.

The next thing that I remember is trying to breathe as I was waking up - I couldn't catch my breath. Then, I realized that I was lying on top of Tom. My shirt was twisted around me, and we were both on the edge of our bed.

"What happened?"

"You passed out."

As Tom explained it, he arrived in the doorway of our bedroom to find me hanging unconscious in my crutches. I had passed out just before he got to the room. He couldn't pick me up under my arms because of the surgery on my right shoulder, and he couldn't pick me up underneath the legs because of my fragile femur. He had turned me around in my crutches, and grabbed me around the stomach. He then pulled me against his body, and guided me back onto the bed, letting me fall on top of him. I specifically remember him telling me later that he lay there, whispering "Please start breathing. Please."

I had never passed out before this night, and didn't know what the stars and the fuzzy feeling meant. Since that night, I have had several experiences that I feel like this, but know now to sit down and rest it out before moving on. I was lucky that night – if I had fallen either way, I would have busted my head – either on the bed or the door. I know that my angels were watching over me.

Learning Our Way...

7/26/01

Contracted Sports Med to set up Roger's therapy for Monday at 4:30. Justin, Jeff, Tom & Boog (Mike) set up the hospital bed for Roger

7:15 pm
Well, in my infinite wisdom, I neglected to finish my past entry of a week ago. I was starting to take medicine that made me sleepy so I didn't really feel much like writing. I saw a dentist, social worker, and a psychologist throughout the day and then the Chaplin came back the next morning.

I was released from the hospital at 10:00 pm on 7/20/01 and got home around 12:30 am going straight to bed. I never really got sick from the treatments – just sick a couple of times. No big deal. Stacy, my R.N., said that would probably be the type of treatment that would be the hardest on me. I really hope so.

Saturday was an amazing day – 50 guys from the area put our house us! It was absolutely amazing. Dave and Linda fed everyone at their garage. I still am so grateful – there is no way that we will ever be able to repay all who helped.

Sunday was an emotional day. There was an accident at the job site with scaffolding and dad injured his knee pretty bad. He didn't break anything but he pulled everything. Allen was also banged up in the fall – but he recovered pretty well.

I just can't believe it happened. Dad's first words were, "Don't tell Ginger..." He was so worried about me. He was really worried about <u>disappointing me</u>! Little does he know, he'll never disappoint me. Anyway, he's okay now, but at the time, we thought he was going to have to have major surgery. It was a hard day to get through – Tom hadn't gotten very much rest at all and had to go to work at 6:00 pm. Jeff & Garret stayed the night with me here at the apartment. They had their own slumber party.

Monday – well, Monday was a crazy type of day. I woke Tom up (an hour after he got home from work) and asked him to make me a piece of toast. I was so hungry and weak, I knew I needed something. Even though I wasn't sick, Tom was really worried about me and wasn't able to get back to sleep after that. Actually, his nerves were starting to kick in from the past weeks events. He was feeling bad about dad getting hurt, kind of feeling it was his fault. He didn't get any rest again and came out at 5:00 pm, really upset. I told him to call work and tell them he wouldn't be in. So, he did and took Monday evening to rest, somewhat. I was feeling okay during the day – I just wasn't eating a lot because I was sleeping most of the day.

That night, Tom slept on the couch and I slept in the bed. He thought we would sleep better that way. Well I got up during the night to go to the bathroom – I was almost back to the bed and I passed out. Tom had to come in and catch me. It scared me pretty bad. I just hadn't eaten enough that day. In addition to scaring me, it really scared Tom. And this just added to his nerves. I was okay, and have been since, but Tom's nerves are pretty shot.

While cleaning out my closet, I found a list of questions that I had written at some point early in my treatment, and just smiled. I knew at the time that these were big issues for my family & I. Looking back, I realize that I learned the answers to these questions the hard way – by living them.

- What Stage? – I wasn't sure if the cancer that I had was diagnosed in stages. I wanted to know how early I was in this thing.
- Vitamins for winter? – You find out during something like this that everyone is a doctor. Everybody has talked to this person, who knows that person who is a nurse at a hospital in a far away city that thinks this and that. One thing that I heard from my resident "doctors" is that it would be a good idea to take vitamins during the winter to help fight off any infections or colds that would be lurking about. Turns out that even the doctor prescribed medicines had a hard time keeping my levels up, but luckily – no infections.
- Date for surgery? – I was anxious to get this date because it gave me something to shoot for. It seems like forever before I found out when it was, but September 26, 2001 was the wonderful day.
- Swelling? –
- MRI? –
- Take Bactrim? – When I started treatments, I was told that I would need to take an antibiotic, Bactrim, every weekend. This didn't make a lot of sense because I was only taking it for two days? Come to find out it was just for a little added help to fend off those nasty infections.

- Go to softball tourney? – I really wanted to go to our local fire department's softball tournament, but wasn't sure that it would be a good idea for me to go up there with all of those people. Turns out, it rained the tournament out and I couldn't go anyway – I was in the hospital with a fever.

7/27/01

Ginger had her first blood tests done at MMH. Her results were: Hemoglobin 13.7 good – white count 2.8 good – platelets 100,000 good – ANC 56 very low should be 500, below 100: no company allowed could pick up fevers or infections. Ginger stayed over night with us while Tom worked. She ate really good.

7/28/01

Ginger spent the day with us. About 7:00 she spiked a fever of 100.3-100.5 at 9:00pm. Tom took her to Columbus to be seen. Roger C. and Gary put the back door on the garage and the small front window in. She was kept and put in room 5324 for 48 hours.

The first trip to the ER was hell. And this was the first of many.

To officially be considered a fever, my temperature had to be at lease 100.3 degrees. Any fever during chemotherapy is a serious thing, especially after the surgery I had been through for my port. A fever could mean infection – and infection in a body with no immune system could be life threatening.

I remember lying in the hospital bed that my parents had placed in their living room that evening. Over the course of that evening, I started feeling tired. My eyelid starting burning and my mouth was like fire. My mom looked at me and asked if I was okay.

"Yeah, why?"

"You're really pale and you have dark bags under your eyes – are you hot?" It must be a maternal instinct – she came over and felt my forehead.

"Ginge, you're burning up."

This was not the news that I wanted to hear. I wasn't sure what this meant for me, but I knew that it meant that something wasn't right. We took my temperature, and it read 100.3 degrees. Now we really didn't know what to do. When I had started treatments, Stacy had given me a binder with questions and answers to "normal" treatment questions. Mom looked in the book and found the answer there – if I developed a fever, I was to call the hospital immediately. We took my temperature again, hoping that it would have went down. The opposite action – it was now at 100.5 degrees. I reluctantly decided to call the hospital.

I had to talk to the doctor on the floor that night, which wasn't my "normal" doctor. This meant that I had to give my entire treatment history to him. He asked my temperature was up to – after I told him 100.5, he told me that I would need to come to the hospital for tests.

After the few days that our family had just had, this was definitely not the news that I wanted to hear.

I remember this "fever trip" over all of the others. I was so scared, and I was so tired – physically and emotionally. I really had no idea what to expect out of this trip, because I had never been to the Emergency Room at Children's before. This was also the first time that I felt the full effects of the chemotherapy and was physically drained – all of my energy was gone. I had never felt this tired before in my life. A family member, while trying to make me laugh, had commented once that if I was told that I could go out and play softball, I could find the energy. The sad fact was that I was too tired to even roll over in bed, let alone run to first base.

After just a few minutes into our two-hour drive to Columbus, I let my emotions go. Other than the day that I talked to the doctor with his grim news, I had never let my emotions show. Being taken up to Children's that night, I cried and felt sorry for myself. I was overwhelmed with the lonely feeling of helplessness – there was nothing that I could do to help my own outcome. I asked that infamous question, "Why me?" I didn't want to go back to the hospital before my next treatment – I wanted to scream and cry and run as far away from the hospital as I could get. I asked Tom why it had to be us doing this – what about all of those people who were so mean and evil? Wasn't I a good enough person? What did I do to deserve this disease? Why was I being tested further with this fever? What if this fever meant that we were going to get even more bad news?

It took a few minutes for me to calm down and re-gain my composure. I knew that I could cry and feel sorry for myself as much as I wanted to, but it was not going to change the fact that I had to go to the hospital to get better – to live. It was also not going to help Tom, or those around me, to help me get through this if I sat around and felt sorry for myself. No one could go through this for me – even though it was offered many times during my treatments – but there is no way that I would let that happen, even if it was possible. By the time that we neared Children's, I was ready to face this night. I had no idea what a challenge it would be.

When we pulled up into the ER entrance, Tom went in the lobby and got a wheelchair for me – I was just too weak to crutch my way into the hospital. I also had to put on a mask before I went into the lobby of the ER. Because of my weakened immune system, any virus floating around in that room could be really bad news for me. I learned quickly that the lobby of the ER was the last place that a cancer patient should be sitting.

Tom wheeled me up to the desk and I gave the receptionist my name.

"We've been expecting you," she said and immediately came around the desk and wheeled me back to my room in the ER. This really surprised me because there were a lot of people waiting to see a doctor, but I was very glad for it. Let me tell you that the "bed" that I had in that room was the most uncomfortable thing I had been on in my life.

They hung masks outside of the door to my room, and the parade of doctors and nurses began, a parade that lasted 4 and ½ hours. I had to give my entire medical history to at least three doctors, explain my diagnosis, why I was there, etc. The scariest of the things that I had to explain was the type of port that I had.

"It's a dual port."

That statement brought a blank look to my ER nurse. This is definitely not the reaction that you want to see on someone that is about to come at you with a needle - especially at 1:00 am in the morning.

"I've never accessed a dual port before. Let me feel it." This led to 10 minutes of the nurse pushing on my port and feeling around, trying to find the perfect spot to pin me with the needle she held in the other hand. This was the last straw for me mentally.

At that point, I had been in the ER room for three hours, and not allowed to take anything for my fever. The ER doctor had told me that I had to have cultures of my port sites taken to make sure that they were not infected. They would need to access both of my port sites to do this culture. I was tired, I was hungry, I was hot, I was uncomfortable, and now I had a nurse pushing a piece of plastic in my chest around and saying, "I think I can do this."

Finally, after changing the gauge of the needles and actually hitting my port on the first try, the cultures were drawn and tested. The doctor came in with good and bad news for Tom & I – GOOD NEWS: the cultures did not show infection, BAD NEWS: I would have to be admitted into the hospital for 48 hours and be given antibiotics to be sure that there was no other infections hiding in my body. At this point, the news that I was going to have to be admitted was not welcome, but I did know that the 5th Floor had more comfortable beds.

After another 45 minutes of waiting for a room to be ready for me, Tom and I were taken to the familiar 5th Floor of Children's and we were able to get some rest.

It ended up that they could never give me a reason for the fevers that I developed – and I would develop a fever after every Doxorubicin treatment that I took. It got to be so regular that I could predict them down to the 30-minute arrival time. The trips to the ER never got better, but I got myself through them. I slowly learned what to say to the doctors and nurses to make them bearable.

Looking back on my treatment, I see the fevers as being thing that made my treatments unbearable. They extended the time that I was in the hospital and made it hard for me to get a break from the reality of my situation. I spent many holidays in the hospital due to fevers and they took a huge mental toll on me.

A New Look...

7/29/01

Tom came home from Columbus at 2:00 pm and my mom & Opal went up to stay and bring her home in a couple of days. She is receiving antibiotics by IV and monitoring her blood count.

7/30/01

Roger started therapy at Sports Med at 4:30. Got a wheel chair for Roger from the VFW in Mtta. from Bob K. and my dad. Ginger was released from the hospital at 1:00. She stayed the night with us.

7/31/01

Ginger stayed with us while Tom worked 6 am – 6 pm. Roger worked 3 hrs at Gress. Kim got us another wheelchair with a prescription from Vienna, WV from Apricia. It costing $2.90/mo. I got Roger's handicapped plaguard.

The good thing about my dad's injury was that he could walk with crutches and still could work a little. He had to do therapy to strengthen his muscles and prepare for surgery, but he could lead a somewhat normal life.

8/1/01

Roger went to therapy at 3:30. Justin took Roger to work at 11:00, left him then to therapy at 3:30. Roger can touch his foot on the floor. Ginger went home, she thinks her hair is starting to fall out.

Up until that day, I had been told that I would lose my hair, but I had always held out hope that it wouldn't. When I started to see my hair on my pillow after a nap, I knew that it was starting to fall out. I would run my fingers through my hair and have a handful of my long, blonde hair when I was finished. I didn't let on that this bothered me at first, but it was an emotion that I couldn't hide for long.

8/2/01
I took Roger to work at 9:00 & Opal picked him up at noon. Tom took Ginger to Columbus for a clinic visit. Her blood count was up over 100 but that's still in the danger zone.

8/3/01
Took Roger to work at 8:30. Roger went to therapy at 12:30.

8/4/01
Ginger came back out to stay until Wednesday when she goes back to Columbus.

8/6/01
Took Roger to Morgantown to see the surgeon, he was doing fine, he'll see him in three weeks again. Ginger had Judy cut her hair off. Me-Shell & Marlene & Denise were here to visit.

This was one of the hardest days of treatment – and, it didn't involve needles, sickness, or physical pain.

After almost a week of finding hair on my pillow and not being able to brush my hair without getting a hand-full of hair, I decided that it was time to let go of my hope that I would keep my hair. It hurt me so much to see the strands falling out little by little. It just seemed to prolong the agony of the inevitable. I knew that it was time for me to cut my hair.

One of the reasons that this hurt so much was that my dad and my Grandpa Chuck had always loved my long, blonde hair. Whenever I mentioned the idea of cutting it, they would both give me a sad look, and I never would be able to follow through on it. This time was different – it wasn't my decision to make.

I told my mom of my decision – I think that the finality of it was just as hard on her as it was on me. We called Judy, a friend who was also a beautician. I just couldn't bear going to a stranger to cut it off – it just didn't seem right. She agreed to do it, and mom and I got in the car for the 10-minute drive to Judy's house. Those 10-minutes seemed like eternity to me. And it was in those 10-minutes that I lost all of my courage to complete this event. By the time that my mom and I pulled into Judy's driveway, we were both crying – sobbing, actually. Neither of us wanted to have to do this. I sat in Judy's chair, crying. Judy decided that we should just cut a few inches at a time. This made it better, not seeing all of my hair being shaved off at once. When we got to just having a few inches left, I couldn't go any further. Judy sensed my hesitation.

"You know, we could just leave it like this. It looks really cute, and it won't weigh as much – maybe it won't fall out as fast this way."

It made perfect sense to me – and my mom. We all agreed to stop where we were. As I looked in the mirror, it was like looking at someone else – I almost looked like a boy. The only thing that looked familiar was my blue eyes looking back at me. But Judy was right - it was cute. I would just have to get used to it.

Driving home that night, mom and I were happy with our decision. When I got home, dad smiled and said that he really liked it, too. I think now that it was easier for us all that way.

People always say that "It's just hair," and they're right – it is JUST hair, and it WILL grow back. But losing my hair was hard for me for a few reasons. First, losing my hair was losing some of my personality. I always wore my hair in a ponytail to play softball, and I loved to curl it when I dressed up to go out. My hair was a part of me that I loved, and I didn't want to give it up – I had already given up so much. It was losing a part of ME.

Second, by cutting my hair off, it was admitting that I was sick. Up until the day that I finally shaved my head clean, I could always "pretend" that what I was going through wasn't serious – maybe just a broken leg or the flu. People couldn't look at me and see that I was sick. But with no hair, it was hard to hide that something was wrong. Shaving my head was like saying, "Okay, you win again, here you go." Although I never backed down from cancer, it felt like a small defeat.

<u>8/7/01</u>

<u>Ginger had local labs done at MMH, no results. Sports Med tried to put Roger on a bicycle to exercise his leg but that didn't go real well. He is bending his leg at 65 degrees; he needs to reach 100 degrees by surgery time.</u>

<u>8/8/01</u>

<u>Tom took Ginger to Columbus to start her second dose of chemo. Roger got his 5% wages back from Gress.</u>

After two days of my "boy-cut," I had had enough. My hair was falling out quicker now, and it was really starting to bug me. Tom knew it was bothering me, and offered to shave it for me. He knew that he could be turned down with this offer, and I think that I surprised him when I said – OK.

We got a nurse to bring a safety razor for us, like the use for surgery prep, and Tom went to work. It took a lot longer than either of us expected, but we got through it all right. When Tom finished, he gave my clean head a rub, I guess for good luck.

I went to the bathroom to look in the mirror – this time, I couldn't find myself in the reflection. With no hair at all, I lost the face that I was used to seeing. This wasn't like a bad haircut, or red hair when you actually wanted blonde. This was no hair – and no going back. The eyes that were staring back at me weren't even familiar to me now. It was a different person in the mirror now. Funny, when I couldn't see my reflection, I was still the same person, but I could see that I wasn't in the eyes of those around me.

It took me a few minutes to clear the tears. When I came out of the bathroom, Tom hugged me and said, "You're still beautiful, blue eyes." It took me many trips past a mirror to finally get used to the person looking back at me.

The Daily Grind...

<u>8/9/01</u>
<u>Septic tank was put in. Roger went to therapy. Ginger was given a surgery date of Sept. 26th and we see Dr. W. on Sept. 18th.</u>

A date for surgery – finally, something to shoot for. I had been through a lot in the past week, and I was glad to get some good news. I looked at surgery as the day that I would be cancer-free. In my opinion, the day couldn't come fast enough.

<u>8/10/01</u>
<u>Roger & Denny put the big window in and the other windows they are all in now. Mom & Opal went to Columbus so Tom could come home.</u>

<u>8/11/01</u>
<u>Salem Ball Tournament. Ginger didn't get to come home, her blood levels were too high from the chemo.</u>

All I wanted was a hot dog and to watch the Sheriff's team play softball. I had played with this team the year before, in this very tournament. We had won, and the team had taken me in as one of their own. This stupid level was keeping me from going. I was feeling great and my blood levels were up – that stupid chemo level was the only roadblock.

<u>8/12/01</u>
<u>Ginger came home at 2:30</u>

Well, by the time that I was allowed to come home, the tournament had been rained out. I missed seeing all of my friends; and the hot dog. Yet another blow. I was feeling like nothing was going to go my way.

8/13/01
Roger went to therapy, his knee is at 81 degrees and he uses only one crutch.

8/14/01
Ginger went to MMH to have labs done. Tom had the tub delivered to the house. Her calcium was low and her electrolytes. Josh & Stephanie came to visit.

8/15/01
Roger had therapy and is walking without crutches. Ginger went to Columbus, Linda S. took her to Columbus, she had her treatment at 7:30, went well. Tom went up Wed. evening.

8/16/01

8/17/01
Tom came home in the afternoon. Roger had therapy.

8/18/01
Opal & Linda Sue went to visit Ginger in Columbus. Her level was .17.

8/19/01

<u>Tom & Ginger's 1st Anniversary, Gary & Carol went to Columbus to visit. Ginger couldn't come home. Tom went up for a couple of hours. Roger and Justin worked on getting the steps to come out right. For some reason the steps were a mind boggler for everyone. Ginger's levels had to be .05 to come home, they were .1.</u>

Our first anniversary – you know that I'll never forget where we spent it. I was so depressed that I would not be able to see Tom. He had worked the night before, and had to work that night, too. There was really no way that he could make the two hour drive to the hospital. Carol and Gary came up to visit, which made the day a little easier to get through. We sat and talked about different items of the day.

All of a sudden, the door opened, and in walked Tom. I could feel an instant smile on my face. He walked to the bed and hugged me so tight – and the tears started to fall. It was so wonderful to see him there. And to get a surprise on a day like that, it was absolutely great.

I had a gift for Tom that day – a Lonestar CD with a song that we both held close to our hearts – "One More Day." The first time that I heard it, it was like hearing a song about our life at that time. I wanted to be sure that Tom knew how I felt about him, and this song seemed to say it all.

Looking back, the day was as perfect as it could have been. Tom couldn't stay very long, but his trip to see me was wonderful. It lifted my spirits, and got me through a rough day. And I know that it wasn't an easy day for him, either. But on that day, we chose to look at the blessings in our lives.

8/20/01
I went to Columbus and picked up Ginger, my mom went along. Her levels were at .06. Opal picked up Roger. I took Ginger to the softball games at Pioneer Park to watch the S.O. play. Bryan gave Ginger his S.O. hat to wear to each game & to wear next year when she plays. Ginger's blood levels were good. Roger's therapy went well.

Finally, I got to watch softball. This night was awesome. My mom had told me that everyone would ask how I was doing, and would always send their best wishes. But on this night, I saw what she meant. The guys would come over between innings and talk to mom & I, and they were genuine with their concern and best wishes. When Bryan gave me his hat, I almost cried. Of course, I couldn't cry in front of those guys, but I felt like I was on the top of the world. He made it very clear that he wanted me to wear it when I *played* next year – that night, I think that there were only two people in the world that believed that I would be playing softball again: Bryan and me. It was good to have someone that believed in my dreams.

8/21/01
Ginger had labs done at MMH. Ginger's labs were at 500 which is low.

8/22/01
Chemo was postponed today because of Ginger's levels being low, her ANC should be at least 750 and they're 500. Steve came down to

the house and showed Tom & Roger what was needed for the electric at the house. Roger's therapy went well.

8/23/01

Ginger had labs done at MMH. Her levels were up, so she'll go to Columbus Friday am. Judy received Ginger's wig, she tried it on and had the bang's cut. It was $173.00.

Well, I'll tell you – if no hair was the worst, this wig was a very close second. It didn't look like me at all, but I was clinging to the security of any kind of hair at this point. I wanted to cry as I sat in the chair that night, in front of my mom and Tom. I wanted so bad for this wig to be perfect – I wanted to see the old me in that mirror. But no matter how much I looked, or how much I pretended, it wasn't me. It looked terrible.

I know that everyone there thought that the wig looked terrible, and could see that I was disappointed with the results, but they wouldn't dare tell me that night. It really would have hurt me more than I could take.

8/24/01

Tom took Ginger to Columbus, started chemo at 6:00 pm. She is in room #4. Roger's therapy was at 85 degrees bend on his leg. Ginger was given a prescription for her wig at the hospital.

8/25/01

Tom came home and Dean & Betty went to visit with Ginger.

I Left it in My Other Jeans...

8/26/01

Ginger came home at 9:30 pm. She was released at 7:00 pm. Carol brought her home. She was sick when she came home and was sick at 2:00 pm. Her prescription for 90 pills to prevent vomiting was $2,500. The hospital finally filled the prescription through in-house meds to file through insurance so she doesn't have to pay for them. She takes one pill every three hours.

The doctor told me that he had a medicine, Zofran, which he would prescribe to help with my nausea – the price of those pills made me re-think how much not puking was really worth. When Tom called me from the pharmacy, he told me the reaction he had when the pharmacist told him the price - "Sorry, I left that money in my other jeans." Gary had been there with him, and his reaction was just as funny – "Wwhat!?"

After I got off the phone with Tom, I paged the nurse, and explained that either they find me something else or I would just have to do without – there was no way that we could afford that price for medicine! After an hour of waiting, the doctor came in with the bottle of pills for me. He explained that they worked it out with the insurance company. I'm certainly glad that it was all worked out – I can't imagine how sick I would have been if I wouldn't have had those pills, but I was prepared to do without.

8/27/01

We went to Morgantown for Roger's visit with the surgeon at 1:15. The trip is 250 miles and it was our third trip. His surgeon scheduled Roger's surgery for Oct. 5th. Ginger has to give herself one shot per day for 10 days and the medication is $256.00/day so the insurance company sent Option Care from Coshocton to the house to bring Ginger her meds. Neupogen 1ml/day.

8/28/01

A nurse from Camden-Clark came out to show Tom, Ginger, & I how to give her shots in her stomach. House calls home health and hospice.

Okay, I've mentioned before that I really hate needles. Now they tell me that I have to take shots, in my stomach of all places, when I'm at home. First of all, there is no way that I am giving myself shots. For the past 24-hours, I had been sweating the idea of giving myself these shots. Now I had a nurse telling me that it was no big deal – just think of it as a dart and sort of stab it in quickly, assuring me that it wouldn't hurt me as bad if I did it quickly.

After only a few minutes of trying to explain it to me, the nurse understood that I was not going to be doing this myself, and turned her attention to Tom and my mom. We figured that one of them would be around at all times, so if each of them knew how to do it, we would have it covered. I could see that my mom wasn't crazy about the whole shot thing, either.

She had Tom practice on me while she was there to supervise the whole thing. He did pretty well, for a rookie! Actually, Tom was a great shot giver – better than the nurses, a lot of the time. It ended up that I would need to take these shots after every Doxorubicin treatment that I took. Tom got to be an expert at giving me the shots. My Grandma Opal even got into the act, and surprisingly, was very good, too.

There was one occasion that Tom bruised me by giving me the shot. When I say bruise, it might bring to mind a black and blue spot about the size of a quarter. Try a black, blue, purple, green, and brown spot the size of a CD. Now, this wasn't because he was rough, or didn't do it right – my platelets were low at the time, and I bruised easily - obviously, very easy. He felt really bad, but it didn't hurt me.

8/29/01
Roger had measurements taken for his new brace at Sports Med. He decided to use his own tendons when he has his surgery, they will use his hamstring and quadriceps tendon to repair his ACL, PCL, & MCL, he'll be in the hospital 3 days and will start therapy two weeks later. This brace costs $925.00.

8/31/01
Ginger had lab work done at MMH and her ANC level was down to 124, low. Roger's therapy went really well.

9/1/01
Tom took Ginger to Columbus at 5:00 am. She had a fever of 102 degrees. Randy V. did the dozer work at the house. Her fever was 103 degrees in the ER, and it came down to 99.8 when she got to her

room. They will take cultures on Sunday and Monday to make sure she isn't contracting anything, if her cultures come back ok on Monday & her temperature stays down, she can come home on Monday (Labor Day.) She is in Rm #10

9/2/01
Ginger had to have 2 units of blood to bring her levels back up. Her ANC is only 150 so she has to stay in the hospital until Tuesday, even though her temp is normal.

I had never received blood before, nor had I ever been around someone that was getting it. But, the paperwork and information that you get from the hospital is enough to scare you out of it. I was thinking about asking if it was really necessary for me to get it.

But I finally got through the stack of forms, and the two nurses who had to look at my admittance sticker to be sure that I was actually the person that the blood was for – and there I sat: eating my dinner with blood being pumped into me. But at this point in my treatment, I had experienced so many things that were out of the norm that things like this were starting to seem normal to me.

9/3/01 (Labor Day)
Roger and I went to Columbus to see Ginger. Her counts weren't up so we couldn't bring her home. Dave put up most of the sulfite and half of one side of siding.

I remember my parents on this day – they were so heart broken that they couldn't take me home with them when they left. It was getting harder to stay at the hospital by myself, and it was hard to see people go home at the end of the day. It made Marietta seem so far away, like another world.

9/4/01
Ginger was released at noon and Tom went to get her and brought here to our house. Ginger had somewhat of a breakdown and so did Roger. It was awful while it was happening but it seemed to help in the long run.

So many things were getting to me, and there was no way to stop it from coming out. As mom mentioned above, it did help in the long run. Everyone got to speak their mind, but in the end, it was better out than in.

9/5/01
Roger started working on two new machines at therapy. It was a close to normal day & evening.

I know that the phrase "normal" isn't so exciting to everyone, but for my mom to write that a day and evening were "normal" was a big thing – believe me, it didn't happen every day!!

9/6/01
Ginger had blood drawn at MMH, her levels were 13,000, it's good. Roger drove to work.

9/7/01

Steve and Dave started the electric work and the concrete in front of the garage was formed. Roger got his new brace at Sports Med. Ginger went to Fort Frye.

9/8/01

The concrete was poured, some siding was put on and they worked on the gas line.

9/9/01.

Ginger came to stay with us until Wed am.

9/10/01

I took my mom to MMH to have surgery done on her left thumb.

Add another family member having surgery!!

Do You Remember Where You Were...

<u>9/11/01</u>
<u>Ginger and Linda Sue left at 7:30 to go to Columbus for clinicals. At 8:00, a hijacked American Airline 747 flew into the American Trade Center in New York City, at 8:05 a second plane took out the second tower at the Trade Center. A plane crashed on the lawn at the Pentagon in Washington D.C. and a plane crashed near the airport in Pittsburgh. America Attacked! 9-11-01</u>

Everyone can tell you where they were when those planes hit, just like they can tell you where they were when JFK was assassinated. I was with my aunt in traffic in the middle of Columbus.

Aunt Linda & I had been talking during the one and a half hour drive into Columbus. I'm not even sure what it was that made me do it, but I reached down and turned up the radio at 8:07am. That's when I heard a newscaster talk about the building being hit by a plane. Then there was a mention about the Pentagon. I couldn't follow the words fast enough – I looked at Aunt Linda, and all I could say was, "What the hell is going on?" We listened in horror, along with the rest of the nation, and learned the truth behind the planes.

We spent the rest of the day in the clinic at Children's Hospital. Every room had a television in it, which was turned to the news. Everyone was walking around in a daze – no one could believe what had happened. How could anyone think of doing this to us?

All I wanted to do was come home – I did not want to be in Columbus, OH. My thoughts were at home with my family. Tom probably hadn't even heard what was going on – he had worked the night before, and was probably sleeping soundly as the world was crashing down around everyone else. I wanted to go home and put my arms around him.

9/12/01

Roger went to Beckley WV on a business trip overnight. Ginger and Tom went to Columbus, she had an x-ray on her knee, chest, CT scan and bone scan, then was admitted in Rm #5 and hydrated for six hours and started her chemo at 9:30 pm.

9/13/01

All of Ginger's test results came back good.

9/14/01

Roger went to Dr's to have his back put in. Therapy went well and Ginger had an MRI done. Tom came home.

9/15/01

Grm. & Grp. Broome had their soup bean dinner. Tom and Roger picked up the plumbing supplies and Roger started on the outside front of the siding. Ginger's levels were at .6 today.

9/16/01

Ginger didn't get home, her levels were .18. Linda Sue and my mom went to Columbus to visit with Ginger.

9/17/01

Dean & Betty picked Ginger up in Columbus, her levels were .09. Roger went to therapy and rode the bike all the way around and he saw his diabetes doctor, everything was good.

9/18/01

We went to MMH to have labs drawn, her ANC was 2303, then we went to Children's Hospital to get Leucovorin at the pharmacy and to see Dr. W. at 2:00. We were told Ginger's surgery will take 4 hours and she will have an incision from her top thigh to her middle calf & staples, she will be in the hospital 4-5 days. She will lose the end of her femur and the top of her tibia. We then met with the anesthesiologist at O.S.U. at 3:00.

9/19/01

Ginger was admitted and hydrated, she still had some traces of chemo so she won't start her chemo until tomorrow. She is in Rm #29,

9/20/01

Bomb threat at Children's Hosp. Started chemo at 3:00 pm after the scare.

Up until this point, all that I had seen on my television was the attacks, and news about the destruction. All of the sadness of the situation had done its fair share of depressing me. I couldn't handle seeing any more of it, so I had turned off my TV, and had stuck my nose in a book.

It's not that I didn't care about what was going on in the world, or that I didn't feel for those who lost their loved ones in those crashes. It was that I was having my own struggles at that time, and the two disasters together were more than I could handle emotionally. In the past few days, I had intentionally distanced myself from the entire situation. But on September 20th, I was brought face-to-face with it.

I was sitting in my bed, bored. I decided that I would turn on the television and watch a movie – the hospital had a really cool channel that played movies 24 hours a day, so I knew that there would be something playing. Flipping thru the channels, the words "Children's Hospital" caught my attention. I stopped at the channel, and read the words "Bomb Threat at Children's Hospital" at the bottom of the screen.

I was stricken with an instant panic – it was that moment that I went from another person watching the television, to a real participant. I then heard an announcement of some "Code" over the intercom system of the hospital. I had never heard anything like this announcement before, and assumed that it was related to the situation - I asked one of the nurses what it meant. When she closed the door, I started to get concerned.

She told me that they weren't telling the patients, so they wouldn't be concerned. The threat was a backpack that was abandoned at the clinic – it was thought to be a bomb. The clinic is where the chemo itself was mixed for patients in the hospital, so everything was on hold until this situation was taken care of. The nurse assured me that everything was going to be okay, and that I was safe.

Finally, the backpack was taken, and it was found that it was not a bomb. But the experience was really unnerving. I decided not to tell my parents about the threat because I didn't want them to worry about me while I was in Columbus. I ended up telling my mom after a while, and she agreed that she was glad that I didn't tell her at the time.

9/21/01

9/22/01
Finished the siding on the house, Uncle Roger, Roger & Tom. Levels were .7 down from 1.14.

9/23/01
Levels were .2. Put up sofit.

9/24/01
Levels were .14 and had to be .1 to be released so she had to stay.

9/25/01
Roger went to Dr.'s for his rib and back. Ginger got out at 2:30. Carol went up and took Ginger to Denny's. Tom went up in the afternoon. The gutters were hung on the house.

Finally, Progress...

9/26/01

Surgery day. We left at 7:00 am (Roger, JR & I) and arrived at 9:00. We had Grm. Opal & Grm. Grosz, Tom, 2 ministers (Linda & Paul) Carol, Kenny & Linda & Dean & Betty. She was to be at the hospital at 9:00 and surgery at 11:00. Ginger actually didn't go to surgery until 1:00 pm. The doctor came out to talk to us at 5:00, she did fine! She'll be up on it tomorrow and home by Monday, a brace for a while. Opal, Tom & I went to Denny W.'s house at 9:00 pm to stay the night. She was in room 742B on the James Wing. She was given blood during surgery.

We had a big group of folks in the waiting room before this surgery. I was extremely nervous, but did my best not to let it show. Some tensions finally came through as tears during a prayer before they took me in for prep. I felt so loved and supported at that moment with everyone around me there. I'm so glad that everyone was there – it really meant a lot to me.

I had finally been taken back to prep, and Tom was with me. They had already taken blood, and had put in the IV for the surgery. After what seemed like forever, they were ready to take me back. In an instant, I was scared. I had been looking forward to this day for a long time, but now it was hitting me – this was a major surgery, a major stepping point in my life. It all really depended on this surgery.

I gave Tom a hug, and they wheeled me out. Going into surgery, they had taken my glasses, so I couldn't see anything but blurs as they wheeled me towards the operating room. I remember waiting outside of the room – it was cold, and the walls were green. There were two nurses with me, and they did their best to talk to me and calm me down, but their conversation turned to what they were going to do that evening. I felt really alone, and wished that I were with everyone in that waiting room.

Soon, they came and wheeled me into the operating room, and I was fast asleep.

I remember waking up in the recovery room after surgery. There were beds all around me, but it was so quiet. I opened my eyes only for a few seconds, and the nurses noticed that I was coming around. The one thing that I remember over everything else was that when I breathed, they were the purest breaths that I had taken in my life. It took me a few minutes to realize that I was still hooked up to oxygen from the surgery. I don't remember how long I was in the recovery room, but it wasn't long before I was being wheeled into my room.

The nurses were getting me comfortable in my room, and I noticed a bald head in the group. "I like your hair cut," I told the nurse. "Very stylish."

It was a double room, but I was the only one there. I sat there, staring at my leg, and all of the wrappings and bandages that covered it. I wasn't sure that I should even move it, so I stayed perfectly still.

Amazingly, I wasn't in any pain. I figured that I would be in a lot of pain after the surgery, and had prepared myself for it.

I also wasn't sure what to do now. I had no idea what time it was, and didn't know where everyone else was. I decided that I would call Gary and let him know that everything went okay, and that I was out of surgery. I don't remember what I said, or what we talked about, but I do know that he was surprised to hear from me.

After a few minutes, I had my first visitors. My mom, dad, and Tom came in the door, and were surprised when I greeted them, fully awake. When they came in the room, they thought that I would still be half asleep from the surgery, but instead, I was sitting there waiting on them to come in. And, in groups of three, my visitors came in and greeted me.

After everyone had gone, it was just Tom, mom, and Grandma Opal in the room with me. I didn't know what to do after the day that we had. The three of them were staying at a family member's home, and could stay a little longer than the rest that were traveling two hours home. They, too, eventually went home, and I sat there alone.

I drifted in and out of sleep that night. I was given a button to push when I was in pain, and the nurses would come in and out to check on me. As anyone who has been in the hospital knows, there really isn't any sleep while you're there.

One of the nurses who were with me during that night will stick with me forever. It is the same nurse that I had commented on his haircut a few hours before. He had been in a few times before, and had always made me feel at ease.

"Ginger, did they tell you that they were going to use any medicine that would show up in your catheter?"

"Um, no, not that I remember – why?"

"Well, your pee is green."

Now that is something that I did not expect to hear from him – "What?"

"Green – like Kermit."

Well, that was enough to break the tension. We laughed for a long time that early morning, which is what I needed. It ended up that it was just some medicine that they had used during the surgery, but it served as a bright spot in my treatment.

9/27/01
The three of us arrived at the James at 10:00 am. Ginger had already been up once and walked around the nurse's station. Beth Worthington was in to visit Ginger. Steve and Dave put the electric in the upstairs yesterday. Ginger took a second trip around the nurse's station at 2:00 pm. The Sheriff's Office (FOP) donated the proceeds of two guns to us and Tom & Ginger. Ginger has a cath and a drain and

<u>she was itching from the Morphine so they changed her pain medicine. I bought Ginger a sachet shell and Justin an Ohio State hat for Christmas. Opal and I left at 5:30, home at 7:45.</u>

The day that I had been waiting for – the day that I walked again. It had been months since I was allowed to put weight on my left leg, and today was the day that I started the process again.

Four physical therapists came into my room much too early for me. But, I was awake, so I told them that I would forgive them. Tom, mom, and Grandma Opal weren't there yet, which I was grateful for. I wanted to try this on my own the first time. Deep down, I was scared that I wasn't going to be able to do it. I didn't want to fail in front of my family – they needed this to be a good thing as much as I did.

The therapists had to work around all of the IV tubes and gadgets that I was hooked up to, and we worked around to get me to set up. As I was getting ready to stand up, one of the therapists asked if I was a swimmer.

"No, I play softball. Why do you ask?"

"You have the most muscular shoulders that I have ever seen. If you're not a swimmer, you should be."

I took that compliment to help build my courage for the next step in the process – the *first* step. As I stood up, it took a few seconds to get my bearings with the new equipment, but I started to get the feel of my knee. I took a deep breath, and then took my first step. Okay, that went okay, so I took another. They weren't pretty, but I was walking, and that's all I cared about. I continued across my room and then back to my bed. I was even feeling good enough to sit in the chair next to my bed. That's where I was when Tom, mom, and Grandma Opal walked in - I'm sure that I was beaming.

Later that day, I walked around the nurse's station to show off my "new" leg to everyone. Of course, my mom cried, but I have to say that I cried with her. I was so proud of how far I had come. I was on top of the world.

9/28/01
Took the cath out, Ginger had some fever last night, not alarmed, took her off the pain killers, was still doing fine.

9/29/01
Took Ginger's drain tube out and walked with one crutch. Carole & Whit visited with Ginger.

This was one of the most painful things in treatment – my leg wasn't bothering me at all – it was the removal of the drain tube that hurt. The fellow that took it out told me to take a deep breath and it wouldn't hurt too bad. He lied.

9/30/01

Dave & Linda, Roger & Bob & Kim went to see Ginger, they took her a sweet gestures bouquet. Dr. W. said Ginger could come home on Monday.

10/1/01

Ginger came home by 2:30, I filled her prescription for Percocet and a laxative at Wal-Mart. Roger had his last therapy before surgery. Roger got his license renewed. Stephanie came to visit.

It was so nice to see Steph – and she came bearing gifts. Ice cream cake – hey, what are friends for? She knew my favorite thing!!

Up until that point, I had strictly forbidden cameras. I did not want my picture taken during this ordeal. This was something that I would never be able to forget, even if I wanted to – I didn't need a picture to remind me of what I looked like, or what I went through. But, I was feeling good that night, and Steph was there. So, when my mom wanted to take a picture of Steph and the cake with me, I surprised even myself by saying yes.

I have to admit that I still cringe when I see that see that picture.

10/2/01

Ginger, Stephanie, & I went to see Bryan at the S.O. Ginger's appetite is back. Gress Equipment is now Leslie Equipment.

10/3/01

Roger's birthday! We had 40 people to see Ginger, and Roger & Tom. Ginger went home to her apartment until Sunday when we get back.

10/4/01

We are going to Morgantown tonight for Roger's surgery tomorrow. Justin is watching the shop while we are gone. No rooms in Morgantown because of WVU weekend.

Five Years...

<u>10/5/01</u>

<u>Roger, Mom & I left the house at 3:00 am and arrived at 5:15 – we were to be in Morgantown at 6:00. Roger's surgery started at 7:30 and was over a little after 1:00 around 5 ½ hours. Surgery went well, they repaired two tendons. Opal, Betty & Linda Sue came at 10:00 and left at 6:00. Mom & I had to sleep in the lounge. The WVU football team were playing at home on Saturday so there were no hotel rooms. He was in room 646.</u>

<u>10/6/01</u>

<u>Roger didn't get to go home, he started therapy at the hospital. Justin & Ginger have their 5th year reunion tonight. Roger has his original leg brace, a pain medicine pump in his knee and a cold-water bladder pump under his ace wrap.</u>

I had looked forward to my 5th year reunion since I graduated from college. I had lost about 25 pounds since graduation, and I had found my true self. I was ready to go to this reunion and not back down from those who intimidated me in high school. It wasn't one of those times when I had planned to seek revenge on those who had make me feel inferior walking the halls at Fort Frye High School – it was a small high school and I was never really a "popular" girl. I just wanted them to realize what they had missed when they had a chance!!

Well, the baldness and knee brace that kept my left leg straight kind of put a damper on the "look what you missed" idea with all of the fellas, but they were not going to dampen my spirits. This was the first time that that I had been out since I was diagnosed – I mean really out. And I wasn't tired – I was excited to be able to walk (okay, step and drag) across the room and not have to sit down to rest.

I had selected my outfit a few days ahead of time, with the help of Stephenie. We had went to the mall, and picked out a gray hat. It was an especially big problem finding pants that will go over my brace, but we finally found a pair of khakis that were big enough. In the end, I looked pretty decent – almost normal. Almost.

The reunion was really fun. I got to see a lot of friends from high school, and everyone asked about how I was doing. It was good to see all of them, and talk to everyone. I went home feeling normal for the first time months. I was finally feeling like a real person – not a pin cushion.

10/7/01
Roger was released at 10:15, we stopped at Wal-Mart for milk and prescription and arrived home at 1:15. Opal had mowed most of the yard. Ginger came out at 5:00 she is emotionally stressed. The US started bombing Afghanistan.

10/8/01
Ginger & Roger kept each other company. I mowed the yard. My dad was cleaning his shotgun in the house and the gun went off.

I knew that my mom was under a lot of stress, and I always tried to ease it for her whenever I could. Tonight, my grandpa's actions were out of my control. My poor mom – she really didn't need anything else to worry about, and here comes this accident out of nowhere.

We talked a lot at night, and I cried to her all of the time. I hope that I didn't add to her stress. I know that tonight, things hit her pretty hard. That night, I wished that I could take all of her worries away.

<u>10/9/01</u>
<u>Ginger had an appointment with Dr. W. in Columbus. She had 58 staples removed and has no cancer left in her knee. Roger had his first shower.</u>

Okay, if anyone ever tries to tell you that removing staples doesn't hurt, smile and nod – and know that they are lying to you to try to make you feel better for the pain that you are about to go through. If it wasn't such a great day for me, I might have cried. 58 bee stings – and not just sweat bees – I'm talking yellow jackets. The nurse was so great – she assured me before she started to remove them that she would take her time, and that we would take a break any time that I needed one. When she said that, I smiled, but didn't think that I'd have to have her stop – I was tough. I mean, I'd been through knee replacement surgery, how bad could it be? Turns out, it was three breaks bad. But, as always, Tom held my hand, and I took a lot of deep breaths – and it was over.

I couldn't help but smile from ear to ear, though. Dr. W. had given me word that all of the margins around the area that the tumor was removed tested negative for cancer. And, they had removed the entire tumor. It was the news that I had prayed that I would hear. My prayers had been answered.

10/12/01
Ginger went to Columbus to start chemo again. She was told she had between 85-90% kill of her tumor. She's in room #28. She was still being hydrated at 8:00 pm. She's in Rm. #29.

My prayers had been answered with news that I didn't have cancer anymore, and that the tumor was mostly dead when it was removed. But my problem now was this – why was I still having chemo? Why did I have to come back and go through this hell if I was already cancer free? I was so tired of the hospital, of the needles, of my bald head. Most of all, I was tired of looking in the mirror and not recognizing the person staring back at me.

10/15/01
Ginger's levels were .18 in the evening. Dean & Betty went to visit with Ginger. The sale of Gress Equipment resulted in Greg, Kathy, Jim, Amanda and Allen losing their jobs today. We are on pins and needles knowing three more employees are going to lose their jobs. Made a trip to Howe's to chat about life.

10/16/01
Terry called Roger at 3:00 to let him know he still has his job.

10/17/01

Ginger came home, Opal & Denny went to get her. She stayed with us.

I Am Thankful For...

Hello. I know that there's a big gap in times between entries, but I sort of decided I didn't want a journal. But I came to a different conclusion a few days ago – a journal will be good for me: a modified version. I'm going to write (at least) 5 things that made me smile during the day. Then I'll add things as I see fit from there.

On September 26th, I had my knee replacement. It wasn't as bad as I had imagined. Rehab is going to be a bear though. I guess walking is my main motivation, Tom is a big help.

Dad had his surgery on October 5th. He's doing good, but is still laid-up.

The house still isn't done. It's causing a big stress for us, especially Tom. It's hard for him to not work on the house and then spend time with me.

Anyway, I think that's all of the updates for now. I'll fill in more as I go.

(this list might be a long one!)
1. Picking on dad
2. Hair growing back
3. Dave and Linda fixing dinner for me
4. Samantha in "spaz-mode"
5. A hug from Tom
6. Being home

7. A leg lift
8. Walking!!
9. Sleeping without my brace
10. Boog – need I say more!
11. Friends you didn't realize you had!

10/18/01
1. "Soup Day" on Third Street Deli
2. Sunshine in October
3. Mozzarella sticks with ranch dressing
4. Singing with the car radio
5. Sam getting a bath
6. Mattress shopping

Tomorrow I go for another treatment – the kind that makes me sick. I'm finding it hard to have a good, strong attitude like before surgery. I'm tired – mentally. Tonight I cried for a long time and complained to Tom about all of the little things I'm missing.

We also discussed my physical therapy. Tom seems to think that I'm not doing enough to walk again. He thinks I don't want it enough. He keeps comparing my rehab to his – and I'm glad he can help me out with his own experiences. I just wish he could see that I'm going through more in my mind right now. It's hard for me to focus all of my energy on walking. There are days, like today, that all I want to focus on is living (somewhat) normal. It's hard for me to explain that to him.

There are a lot of things to talk about – what I've been through, what I've learned, people I've met, ideas I've had, etc. I'll have plenty of time to discuss them.

Until next time…

When Tom was 16, he was in a car crash that could have easily taken his life. Instead, he had to have his right hip completely rebuilt. Tom can do everything pretty normally, even walking without a limp and running. It was great that he knew what I was going through with this, but it was hard to compare the two rehabs.

10/19/01
Ginger went back to Columbus for her bad chemotherapy – started hydrating her and started her treatment at 8:00 pm

10/21/01
I went to Columbus and picked up Ginger after I got off work. She was sick in the morning before we picked her up, when we got home and at 6:00 am Monday.

10/22/01
I took Roger to Morgantown for his follow-up visit after surgery and to have his stitches taken out. We go back 11/10/01 and he goes to therapy. Ginger started taking her shots in her stomach again. I decided to start Ginger a book of letters from her friends for Christmas. I made 31 phone calls.

1. Mom taking care of me when I'm sick
2. Lifting my leg without my brace
3. Talking with Grandma Opal
4. Knowing God loves me – bald and crippled!!
5. Nurses that take care of me
6. Meeting people who have the same thing I have and are almost done!

I have been in the hospital getting "the bad" chemo so I didn't feel much like writing. I'm home (at mom and dad's) now. I feel pretty good right now, considering I usually feel pretty crappy. They changed the med's that I'm taking, so maybe it will help me feel better sooner.

I guess I don't have much to write about. I met a couple of kids who are almost done with chemo and that makes things good: to know I'll eventually be there, too.

We'll talk again soon!

<u>10/23/01</u>
<u>Roger went back to work, went fine other than his back hurt a lot. Stopped giving him too much potassium, hope he starts to feel better</u>.

1. Sleeping on my stomach
2. Watching TV with Grandma Opal
3. Doing exercises with Tom
4. Walking without my brace for the first time
5. Dad after he takes pain medicine – "Loopy"

6. Lifting my leg into bed without help

Finally! I'm improving on my physical therapy exercises. So Tom & I decided that I could try to walk without my brace. It felt really good. Tom told me that I was doing good – the praise from him felt good. I'll be going down to the apartment and I'm looking forward to spending an evening with him. I seem to feel happier and smile when he's around.

Imagine – being happier when I'm around my husband. He lifts my spirit – makes me laugh. I don't know how I'd do it without him. Actually, I don't know how I'd do without all of my family and friends. I cry to mom almost every night during my stay here. Maybe it helps her, too, to be able to say what's on her mind.

Dad seems to still be taking this whole thing bad. He cries a lot and his stomach bothers him: I think it's his nerves. He worries a lot. Today was his first day of work since his surgery.

10/24/01
Roger started back to therapy, bent his leg 40 degrees to start. Ginger went home.

10/25/01
Cleaned Ginger & Tom's spare room. JR passed his state teaching boards.

How To Say Thank You...

October 26, 2001

I sat at the computer and tried to think exactly what I would want Tom to know if I didn't make it out of this situation. I knew that I couldn't tell him face-to-face. Not that I wasn't able to say thank you, but I knew that Tom thought that what he was doing wasn't anything that anyone else wouldn't do. But I knew different – some husbands would have left in a heartbeat. Every time that I would try to say how wonderful he was and that I appreciated everything that he did, he would just brush it off, like it was nothing. I thought that I would write a letter, even if I didn't give it to him. That way I would be able to say what I was thinking, but wouldn't have to "embarrass" him by bringing it up.

That's what I was thinking when I wrote this letter. I never gave it to Tom. I just couldn't find the right time, or the right way to introduce it to him. I didn't know how he would react to it, but I never deleted it either. I thought some day when we were old and gray, I would give it to him, maybe on our anniversary. Whenever I gave it to him, I wanted it to be special to him. I hope it is.

"October 26, 2001

Tommy,

I don't know when I'll finish this letter and I'm not sure when I'll give it to you. It might be tonight, or maybe a few months down the road. I can't always say what I'm thinking without breaking down and crying, which really doesn't help me to get my point across to you in the right way. I hope that you can understand what I'm thinking in this letter.

First of all, I want to thank you for keeping my life somewhat "normal" through all of this. I feel like I can tell you anything and say exactly what I'm feeling at the time. You don't know how much that means to me. You know, I really don't know how you do it. Trips to the Double L and just going out makes me see what I'm missing and why I'm getting better again. The trips give me something to smile about while I'm sitting in my private room in Columbus – and gives me something to look forward to again.

There is no way in this world that I will ever know how you have felt, or are feeling during this crazy time. Everyone asks me how you are doing, and I have to tell them fine because that's how I see you. I don't want you to think that you have to bottle up your feelings when you're having a hard time, or feeling a little depressed. Some times it makes me feel better to help someone else through their own feelings. It's not fair of me to ask you to take in all of my grief and misery and not share in helping you through yours, and I am more than willing to be there for you – anytime. I actually wish that you would talk to me a little more about your feelings – I start to worry about you when you don't let me know what you're thinking.

Sometimes I wonder how long it will take me to get back to the way I used to be. (I guess we can safely assume that I'll never be exactly the way I used to be, but you know what I mean.) I can't wait until we can start doing the things we were supposed to already be doing. I guess we've never been an ordinary couple though, have we? It might not be the same, but we can believe that it will be better. What have we learned from this whole thing? How can we apply it to our daily relationship? I guess we'll find out.

Since July, I have experienced more love in my life from you than most people experience in their entire lifetime. I have definitely been blessed by the love of a husband who loves me for who I am. You make me feel beautiful - like I am the most beautiful thing you have ever seen. The strength of your love comes through in every single little thing you do for me. I see how much you care in all of the things that you do (and probably think I miss you doing.) To hug you is pure heaven and to have your arms around me is something that I miss more than anything. Your arms are the safest place for me, the most comfortable spot to be. You have been my waiter, my bather – anything I have ever asked for.

Sometimes I wonder how I am going to pay you back for the love you have shown these past months. I know I'll spend my entire life trying. I don't think that I can ever show you exactly how much you mean, I can never say I love you enough. I see so many other couples going through the dumbest little things and wonder how I am so lucky to have you. What did I do to deserve you? Why am I so lucky? You have rescued me so many times, even before this. Sometimes, I'm not sure how you put up with me. All I know is that you are my best friend.

I want to be everything you have ever pictured a wife to be. I want to make your life wonderful and happy every second, every day. I want to be so close to you, you'll probably get sick of me. I picture spending an entire week with you, cuddled up in our new bed (in our new house, of course) and talking like we used to. I want to have those music nights we used to have and the nights to talk about whatever we feel like until 2:00 in the morning. We learned so much about each other during those times, and I think that we still have more to learn. (Of course, now we might have to share some bed space with Sam, but she normally doesn't take up too much room!)

I still don't know what I want to do next year after this is all over. I guess I've learned to value the boring, normal city life. I wouldn't be against going out on the weekends and spending a bunch of time with our friends. There is one thing that we need to make sure that we do – make time for the two of us. Maybe once a week, we make a deal that we have our own night for just the two of us. I know that this might not always be do-able, but I want to make sure that I spend time with you, and not have to share you with other people. I might turn a little selfish with you, but can you blame me? I don't want you getting away from me, especially after you have put so much time into me!!"

This letter explains my feeling about Tom – then and now.

No Rest...

10/27/01

Took Roger to the E.R. in Morgantown after his incision burst open, they took cultures and blood work, gave him IV antibiotics and sewed his leg shut without numbing it. We came home at 6:00. It was trick or treat. He is taking Keflex, an antibiotic.

10/28/01

Had Opal's 64th birthday party at 4:30. Roger's leg was still draining some. Ginger started a fever while she was here. It was 100.3 and 101 degrees. Room #26.

10/29/01

Took Roger back to Morgantown to see his surgeon. His test results were okay. We go back in a week.

10/30/01

Ginger's levels came up from 0 to 28, still really low. They gave her platelets, the white cells of the blood, instead of giving her blood. Roger's leg stopped seeping in the evening.

10/31/01

Halloween, Ginger came home from Columbus – she took more platelets. She may have a lower bowel infection.

11/1/01

Roger is feeling poor, actually worse every day since Monday.

11/2/01

Ginger had labs done and her count was back up to 6000. She is feeling good and taking antibiotics for a rectal infection. Roger had a better day today.

11/3/01

Roger's leg bled again. I took the wheelchair back to Lowell.

11/5/01

We went to Morgantown to see his surgeon, leg still bleeding. Ginger had labs done again at MMH, her hemoglobin was low but other levels were good. The doctor put 3 strips on Roger's leg and he can go without his brace. We go back in a week.

11/6/01

Ginger went to Columbus, Opal took her. She started hydrating at 10:00 am. She received four units of blood. Roger's leg is still bleeding. He had a good talk with John L. Ginger weighed 142 pounds this week. She has to wait 72 hours after her blood before she can come home. She has some hearing loss.

The diagnosis that I had lost hearing upset me more than I let on to my family. This was an unexpected side effect from the chemo – I had no idea that I might lose hearing. It wasn't a big percentage that I had lost, I guess it was just the idea that there was no getting it back once I lost it.

11/8/01

Kim brought some steristrips home to put on Roger's leg because the others came off.

11/10/01

Ginger's levels were at .19. Put up outside Christmas lights.

11/11/01

Ginger came home, her levels were .06 finally. She has 82 degrees of movement in her leg.

11/12/01

Took Roger to Morgantown and the surgeon cauterized his incision to close it so it doesn't bleed any more. Took labs at MMH and they were good.

11/13/01

Took Ginger to Columbus for her last bad chemo. She is in Room 17. She had an EKG done, she had a difference in her rhythm of the Q-T segment. She has had some fast heartbeats when she's at rest. Types of chemo – Methotrexate, Doxarubicin, and Cisplatin (make her have fevers and vomit) will have to take shots in her stomach again, GCSF shots.

From the beginning of this, I had heard some scary things: 1) You have cancer. 2) You will need to have a knee replacement. 3) You will never be able to play softball again. Now this: Prolonged QT. It didn't seem like much when they were first explaining it to me, but I thought that it was odd that they were asking me so many questions. I continued to think that it was nothing until I was visited by the head of the cardiology department, on a weekend no less. It happened to be a weekend that no one was in the hospital with me, and no plans on coming up for at least two days.

The cardiologist explained that it was not definite that I had this condition, but that if I did, there were a lot of things that I was going to have to avoid: one being physical activity. If I did have this heart condition, any rise in my heart rate could result in instant death.

I didn't hear anything that the doctor said after this – I wasn't listening any more. I was in such a strange place right now – they tell me that the chemo that I had been taking to cure me of cancer has given me a heart condition that could kill me instantly if my heart rate would rise. How was I supposed to feel about this? Was I supposed to be grateful that the chemo had cured me? How was that possible, when the life that it was trying to give me would be less of a life because I could never have any activity in it? I can't even watch a baseball game without my pulse rising. And why hadn't they told me that this was a side effect? Why didn't I have a choice in this?

The biggest mistake that I made during this situation was not the panicing – I called my dad and told him everything that the Cardiologist had just told me, including the instant death part. While he sounded fine on the phone, I found out later that the minute he hung up the phone, he broke into instant tears. He was so upset – daddy's little girl was sick, and he couldn't fix it this time. I wished that he could make it better – all I wanted at that time was a hug from him.

After many days of worry, and many EKG's, it was found that I did not have the prolonged QT condition – the irregular readings on my tests were caused because of my levels of electrolytes, not my heart. A lot of worry for no reason.

11/14/01
Roger went back to therapy her started at 48 degrees and 58 degrees on the machine, his leg bled some, the scab came off. Ginger is at 85 degrees bend with her leg.

11/15/01
Kim checked Roger's leg and decided to call the surgeon on Friday.

11/16/01
Ginger came home, she had been sick three times, but nauseous a lot. The surgeon wants us to go to Morgantown at 8:00 tomorrow, leg still bleeding.

11/17/01
Went to Morgantown to have the surgeon reassess Roger's leg again. He had blood work done at Mon. General for surgery on Tue. or Wed. of this coming week. They will call us on Monday. Roger passed out after having his blood drawn. It took 2 doctors, 3 nurses, and me to get him on a cot and to start breathing again.

11/20/01
Roger came down with a sinus flu, took him to Howe's – he was given a shot of penicillin and a shot of Decadron. Ginger had labs done at

MMH and her levels were good. They started dry walling the ceilings – Matt W.

11/21/01
Tom and Ginger signed loan papers at the bank. Roger went to work with his sinus flu and he went to Sports Med after work.

While the building of the house was big in the minds of most of those around me, it had taken a back seat for me. It wasn't that I wasn't excited about it, or appreciative of what my family and friends were doing for Tom and I – it was the fact that I couldn't be there and be involved in the work that was being done. It was too dusty for me to go and even look at it. I could just imagine what it looked like. It was really hard for me not to be a part of something that was a big part of my future.

Getting Tired...

<u>11/22/01 – Thanksgiving</u>
<u>Roger wasn't feeling much better but he went to mom & dad's for dinner at 6:30. Ginger was too weak to come to dinner and at 7:00 she called with a fever of 101.3 degrees so her and Tom went to Columbus.</u>

The day that I was looking forward to most for the previous 2 weeks was Thanksgiving. I was feeling good, and knew that I wouldn't be sick from Doxo at the time. The one thing that I didn't predict was the fever. 30 minutes before we were supposed to leave for Thanksgiving dinner, I started feeling hot. I knew that there was nothing that I could do to prevent it, either.

We called my mom and told her the news that we were on our way to Columbus, and not my grandma's for dinner. I was heart broken. Mom and Aunt Linda brought Tom down a plate of Thanksgiving dinner before we left, and helped me pack for the trip. Over time, I had learned that the three days of a fever trip were long and boring – I packed many things to keep me occupied.

I wouldn't cry in front of my mom and aunt because I knew that this was as hard on them as it was on me. But, once I got into the car, I let my tears go. It wasn't like the turkey meant a lot to me, it was the idea that I couldn't enjoy my life like everyone else. I had to force myself to remember that by missing this holiday, I was helping to ensure that I got to enjoy many holidays in the years to come.

11/23/01

Roger had to go to Physicians Care for his flu. Ginger was taking platelets and her ANC was at zero. She is having an EKG done again because she has pains in her back. She is in room 15.

11/24/01

Ginger was on a heart monitor for precautions from her pains in her back. Her electrolytes were low so she was taking potassium, zinc and magnesium again. Her bowels were full and causing her pain. Roger still has his coughing and some vomiting after his sever coughing. Kenny, Jeff and Justin moved the hospital bed back to Mom & Dad.

One of my mom's goals was to have the hospital bed out of the living room before Christmas so that we could put up the Christmas tree in there. Today, one of her goals were met. It's the small things in life that make it worth living.

11/25/01

Ginger came home from her stay at Children's from her Fever on Thursday.

11/26/01

Roger lost the scab on his leg finally!! We all got together and put up the tree.

It has always been a tradition for my mom and I to put up the Christmas tree together – it meant a lot to both of us to be able to continue this tradition. I also put the angel on the top of the tree, with Tom's help. My mom, being the camera bug she is, had to snap photos of Tom holding me by the straps of my bibs that I was wearing that night. I know that it sounds strange, but it was a perfect night – a tradition that I could be a part of continuing.

11/27/01

Took Roger to therapy and to Howe's for his sinus flu for the 3rd time, he's had it a week now. Ginger was scheduled for treatment today but her levels were too low. Roger graduated from a crutch to a cane at Sports Med.

11/28/01

Ginger had labs done at MMH and her platelets were still too low – they were 42 and should be at least 75, so no chemo this week.

11/30/01

Roger drove himself to work and can now shower & dress himself. We are on our way to a normal life again.

12/4/01

Ginger went to Columbus for her chemo. She is in room 5321 but will be moved to another room. Her counts are high.

12/5/01

Ginger was moved to room 18. She was depressed.

12/7/01

Ginger's levels are .41. Dean and Betty went to see her.

12/8/01
Ginger's levels were at .27. Roger bent his knee to 93 degrees on the machine.

12/9/01
Ginger's levels were .14 and she still had to stay.

12/10/01
Roger & I went to Morgantown to see his surgeon. He was doing fine, he can use a cane now instead of a crutch. He has therapy orders to gain 20 degrees in the next four weeks when he goes back to see the surgeon. Ginger came home at 1:30, her levels were .08.

If you notice, my counts moved slowly – very slowly. This was always a difficult admission for me mentally. Depression would often set in during these long, boring days. It was during these times that I learned that loneliness was harder to deal with than chemo a lot of times.

An Outpatient...

12/11/01

Ginger went to Columbus to take her first outpatient chemo – Doxorubicin. Her counts have to be 750 and they were only 756, she just made it because of the accumulation of chemo in her body. Her hemoglobin levels are low, which makes her look and feel tired. She is taking leukovorin again, she can stop taking it when her count is .05, it is .06 now. Her heart echo and EKG came back okay.

12/12/01

Ginger went back to Columbus for her second day of outpatient chemo.

I had completed the Cisplatin treatment of my protocol, and could now come to the clinic and take the Doxorubin treatments. It was good to come home and sleep in my own bed. By this time, I learned that the more time I could spend away from the hospital, the better I would feel – at least emotionally. I knew that the fevers would still come, but there were more nights that I could sleep in my bed, and that was wonderful.

12/13/01

Took Ginger to lunch and shopping, and out to eat. Her levels were 1100 from her tests on Monday.

12/20/01

Ginger went to Columbus for her follow-up visit with Dr. W. and for labs at Children's, when she saw Stacy they decided to do a short term admit to give Ginger blood to boost her hemoglobin level and give her an IV of magnesium to bring up her electrolytes. I called Opal to inform her, went fine. Roger is up to 102 degrees on the machine, and 82 degrees naturally.

12/21/01
Ginger had to stay in Columbus until 8:30am. She had 3 ½ units of blood and the platelets gave her hives, so they had to observe her longer. She was actually more sick than she had ever been, vomiting and fever. Blood takes 2 hours per unit. Ginger has tendonitis in her knee, at least she has a tendon. He gave her Viox to take, but she isn't going to take it because it slows down the excretion of Methotrexate. They took x-rays and Ginger has copies. Ginger started having a fever at 4:00pm of 100.5, by 5:30 it was 101.9, so Tom took her back to Columbus. They had only been home for nine hours.

This is a day that I will never forget – it was complete hell. When they admitted me for the blood transfusion, Tom and I had tried to explain to them that they might as well keep me because I would be developing a fever the next night – of course, they wouldn't listen. Because my platelets were low, they decided that they would give me a bag of those, and we ended up spending the night in the hospital. During the middle of the night, I became violently sick. When I say sick, I mean the worst vomiting that I had endured during my entire treatment. I was miserable with hives and fever. Tom just sat there, rubbing my back – he knew that this was as bad as I had ever been. They tested me to see if I had had a reaction to the platelets, but the tests came back negative. I'm not sure what it takes to be an official reaction, but let me tell you that it was definitely some kind of reaction.

They sent me home at 7:00 am that morning, and I developed a fever at 4:00pm. I was totally exhausted from the ordeal that I had been through the night before, so another 2-hour drive to Columbus, and 4-hour ER visit completely drained me. The nurses, I mean angels, on the 5th floor took pity on me and postponed my morning vitals so that I could get some sleep. Without those wonderful ladies, I would not have been able to get through it.

12/22/01
Ginger still has a fever of 100.6. Her cultures came back negative. She has to be in the hospital 24 hours after her fever came down.

12/23/01
Ginger still had a fever until noon. We are hoping she gets to come home on Christmas Eve.

The Holidays...

<u>12/24/01 – Christmas Eve</u>
<u>Ginger got to leave the hospital at 3:30.</u>

I have to say that Children's Hospital is a magical place during Christmas. I was showered with gifts from so many different people – I came home with three bags of toys!! There were even a few families of past patients that brought gifts to the rooms. It was wonderful because they knew better than anyone what the patients were going through.

They try to get everyone home that they possibly can for the holiday, so they let me go home. They told me that if I could feel I had a fever on Christmas Day that I would need to come back up to the hospital. I assured them that if I took my temperature and had a fever, I would be back. The minor detail that I didn't tell them was that I had no intention of even taking my temperature. I set my mind to enjoying the day.

One of the greatest gifts that I have received in my life was the book of letters that my mom compiled for me. The book had around 50 letters from family and friends, telling me about how they felt about my cancer and treatment. Many of the letters came from people that I hadn't talked to for a very long time – teachers, high school friends, old neighbors – even the baseball coach from college had written a letter. This book, and its many letters, provided me with much needed inspiration for the rest of my treatment. I hope that everyone who wrote me a letter knows how much that I appreciate it, even today. I can open that book at any time and I still cry at the wonderful words of inspiration in those letters.

One of my favorite poems in my mom's book of letters was a poem from Melanie, one of my former neighbors. I had babysat for her children, and our families were pretty close. This poem followed a really great letter that told the story of my life through her eyes – it sounded pretty good!!

I was a member of the Relay for Life Steering Committee for Washington County in 2003. One on my duties was working on the luminary service, a special event for me. We met one day and were brainstorming about what we should include during the service. We wanted something special and different for the survivors that were there – something inspirational and that told the story of a survivor. I immediately thought of this poem. They asked me if I would read it during the ceremony, and I accepted.

"Donkey's Wisdom

One day, a farmer's donkey fell down into a well. The animal cried piteously for hours as the farmer tried to figure out what to do. Finally he decided the animal was old and the well needed to be covered up anyway. It just wasn't worth it to retrieve the donkey. He invited all his neighbors to come over and help him. They all grabbed a shovel and began to shovel dirt into the well.

At first, the donkey realized what was happening and cried horribly. Then, to everyone's amazement, he quieted down. A few shovel loads later, the farmer finally looked down into the well and was astonished at what he saw.

With every shovel of dirt that hit his back, the donkey was doing something amazing – he would shake it off and take a step up. As the farmer's neighbors continued to shovel dirt on top of the animal, he would shake it off and take a step up. Pretty soon, everyone was amazed as the donkey stepped up over the edge of the well and trotted off.

Life is going to shovel dirt on you, all kinds of dirt. The trick to getting out of the well is to shake it off and take a step up. Each of our troubles is a stepping-stone. We can get out of the deepest wells just by not stopping and never giving up. Shake it off and take a step up!!"

<u>12/26/01</u>
<u>Justin took Ginger back to the hospital, they left at 8:00, she in room 25. They started Metho chemo at 8:00 pm.</u>

<u>12/28/01</u>
<u>Opal & Denny went up to see Ginger in the AM, Dean & Betty went up to see her in the afternoon.</u>

<u>12/29/01</u>
<u>Ginger's levels were .9 in the am, and .4 at 10:00 pm. Roger and I went up to visit when I got off of work.</u>

12/30/01

It's funny, mom had written the date down in her notes, but no description. I can only assume that she fell asleep before she got to write the details of the day. I'm sure that she deserved the sleep – I can hope that it was peaceful...

12/31/01
Ginger's counts were at .17 in the am, and she was released at 11:00 pm – her counts came down to .09.

1/1/02
Justin fell at work and had to be taken to the ER from the Lafayette. He had 30 stitches from falling on a flooded floor in his left knee.

All I can say is, when it rains, it pours.

1/3/02
Opal took Ginger to Columbus for her chemo treatment. Roger went to see his diabetes doctor and everything was fine. He'll go back in 4 months. Roger finally got to get his leg to ride the bike clear over in therapy.

1/4/02
I took Ginger to Columbus for chemo. She bought another wig, a short one this time.

1/5/02

We had everyone's birthdays in January party at 7:00 and our anniversary. We had 17 people Scott (Scoot) wrote a song for Ginger and sang it to her while he played his guitar during the party.

A New Year...

1. Club House Grill at Applebee's
2. flannel sheets
3. sleeping in
4. Sam sleeping with me during the day
5. getting out of the apartment

January 8, 2002
1. A day to relax
2. Sam picking on Tom
3. help with laundry and dishes
4. phone calls from family
5. funny birthday cards
6. plans when they start to come together

1/9/02
Today is Ginger's 24th birthday

1/10/02
Ginger got a fever 100.5 all of her counts were low her ANC was only 14, her hemoglobin was 6.9, they should be 10. She had to go to Columbus for blood and to get her fever down. Roger got his new truck at McConnelsville. Ginger was in Rm #27.

1/11/02
Our 16th Anniversrary, $20 from my parents, $20 from Opal & Denny, Dan Seals cd from JR. Justin's stitches were removed.

Children's Hospital, room 26
1. *my bed at home*
2. *children's movies*
3. *mom and dad celebrating another anniversary*
4. *Grandma Opal caring so much*
5. *Boog heating up a bowl of soup when I'm tired*
6. *My birthday – another year to live*
7. *house plans that continue to go our way*
8. *nurses who really care*
9. *a full night's sleep (can't wait) on our new bed.*

I'm sitting here in my hospital bed at Children's. Grandma Opal left earlier after bringing me up to the ER with a fever last night. Tom is working on the house and will be up tomorrow. Not much on TV, so I decided to write. Currently, I am bald, my stomach is bruised from a shot, my knee is bothering me, my butt hurts – blisters and sitting too long, and my back bothers me. Oh – I'm pretty bored, too.

<u>1/12/02</u>
<u>Ginger was released at 10:00 pm We went to dinner at the Mtta Legion with friends. Peg & Randy gave us a lantern.</u>

January 14, 2002
1. *remembering to write in this journal*
2. *my butt feeling better*
3. *Tom going out of his way to buy me a CD (Jodee Macena – Burn)*
4. *The phrase "you can go home" coming from a doctor's mouth*

5. The end of February is always getting closer ☺
6. All of Carries tests coming back negative
7. House plans that, for some reason, have still gone our way (Knock on wood!)

I'm finally home from my fever trip to the hospital, and I'm having "one of those days." I am still REALLY bored. There is nothing for me to do during the day since everyone is at work at that time. This whole house thing is about to drive me insane (and Tom, too!!) Everyone has their own opinion about what needs to be done and how it needs to be done. I'm sick of this! I cannot wait until Tom & I can settle down in our own home!! I'm sure Tom has the same feeling – maybe stronger. He has been asked to do more in the past 7 months that anyone should be asked to do in their lifetime. He is my hero.

January 15, 2002

1. Tom keeping me sane
2. Getting my last shot!!
3. Getting paid
4. Listening to music with Tom
5. Going out to see my house (so I know what it looks like with my own eyes!)

A day from hell – that's what I'll say it was! Actually, it was all about "normal" life – not complications from treatment. I am thankful for that. Oh well – we're almost there. We're moving next Saturday!

1/16/02

Ginger had labs done at MMH but her levels weren't good enough for her to have her treatment tomorrow, so she will have labs done again on Monday. They had carpet laid upstairs yesterday.

1. One day closer to moving in
2. Finding money in our checking account
3. Sam being absolutely adorable
4. Sleeping in
5. Finally getting out of the apartment

1/21/02

Ginger had labs done and they were good enough to go to Columbus on Tuesday. Roger went to Morgantown to see his surgeon, he has 97 degrees of bend and he goes back Mon. March 11, at 2:30. Ginger is having trouble with her feet going numb. They will do an MRI and leg x-ray tomorrow. All the tests came back good.

1. A few days away from Columbus
2. Finding out you don't owe medical bills
3. Being "almost" ready to move in
4. Jeff's team winning a game
5. Bruises healing
6. Only 5 more admissions!! (2 treatments + 2 fevers + 1 surgery)
7. Sam in "spaz-mode"

You know, I definitely believe in the phrase "when it rains, it pours." Everything was going so well, but yesterday morning, Tom pulled something in his back while turning over in bed. He's in a lot of pain. We took him to the doctor this afternoon. They said they don't think it's serious, but he's still in a lot of pain. I think he's going to sleep on the living room floor tonight. I hate to see him hurting, especially since he's been taking such good care of me. I've been trying to ask him if there's anything he needs, and take good care of him, but it just makes him mad. I don't know what to do to pay him back for being so wonderful to me all this time. Life just doesn't seem fair, at least not recently. We're supposed to move into the house Saturday and I'll probably be in Columbus, and Tom's back is hurting. I wonder why we're being tested like we are. I guess it's not my place to ask. I don't ever feel like myself anymore. This week is Week 28 – 7 months of this torture, of life just being something I can't have. 7 months of learning about blood and diseases that I never wanted to be a part of. You know, I always went through my life before, living as I seen right and following my conscience. Never in a million years did I ever believe I would get sick. Never thought I would get cancer. Never imagined I would need a knee replacement. Couldn't see I'd have to put my dreams and life on hold. And you really wouldn't think that the further I went into treatment and the closer I got to being finished with treatments, the more bitter I become. I can't get my mind and my spirit straight. I can't get excited about life again, it's like I'm scared about what to do. I thought I lived life right before and look what happened. What can I do to make sure I won't get sick again? How can I ever feel safe again? Plus, I have been told by many people that I'm their hero. What do I do about that? I don't know how to live up to that title! Can I ever be the person I used to be? The wife I wanted to become? The mother I dreamed of being? Now who do I want to be? What are my dreams for the future? How do I want to make my mark in this world? Are these things really up to me in the end?

I guess I'll never know that answers to these questions, not in this life anyway. Maybe I don't want to know. That's how it's supposed to work anyway. I guess life isn't all that complicated – you go with it until it stops: then, hopefully, you get the answers. Like they say, pain is temporary.

*I set back and try to collect the things I've learned during this whole ordeal. *Faith is some times all you have to hold onto *You don't have to be related by blood to be considered family *Loneliness can be worse than physical pain *Things don't always go the way you had planned. *You are stronger than you ever thought possible. You just won't realize it until you're tested *More people care than you would ever imagine *Life is never normal or routine.*

This isn't all I want to say, but it's getting late and my hand is cramping. I'll write more later.

<u>1/22/02</u>
<u>Ginger had a treatment today and stayed thru Mon., Jan. 28th. .09 at 6:00 pm.</u>

Love...

January 23, 2002, Children's room 5313

1. Tests coming back negative
2. Getting our new phone numbers
3. Most of all, Tom feeling better
4. Getting compliments on my wig
5. Actually getting a comfortable bed
6. Memories of me and my Grandpa

Today would have been Grandpa Chuck's birthday. The 16th of the month made 5 years since he's been gone. There are days that I still can't believe he's gone. Once in a while, my sink in my room will turn on for no reason – there's no one in the room, no one around, but it just comes on. I always think its Grandpa, letting me know that he's here, watching over me, telling me I'm not alone. I know he's been beside me during this whole thing. I believe that God has a plan for everyone and He has a reason for everything He does, but I will never understand why He took Grandpa from me – from my family. Boy, I wish he were here now. I would love to see those beautiful blue eyes smiling at me. Paw taught me so much, especially to love and trust in God. I know that it has been that love and trust that has got me through this whole ordeal. I know they're both here with me now, and always...

I'm missing Tom pretty bad. I think that it's just because I know he won't be up this visit. Plus, I watched a wedding show last night. It *reminded me of our magical day and made me miss him even more. He has been so brave, so wonderful during this whole thing. It seems so unfair that we didn't get to complete our newlywed status. But I will say I think that our love has grown stronger and deeper. The past 7 months definitely have not been about sex. We have spent more time apart since this has started. We've built a home during this ordeal. Some how, Tom has found a way to provide me with more support and more love than I ever imagined possible. I think that he will need a long time to actually come down from the adrenaline and nerve rush that has got him through this. He has never asked me for anything. He hasn't cried on my shoulder, even when I offer it to him. He has always referred to this as a "bum in the road." Everyone has said I have so much courage and strength. I guess it's because I'm the one that physically goes through it. But I wish people would look at Tom and see how strong and brave he is. How much he has been through and how hard this has been on him: to find out 11 months into his marriage that his new wife had cancer, to have all of his plans and hopes for the future put on hold. He had/has the pressure of being the sole provider for the home, my nurse, construction worker and homemaker. All the while, being supportive and romantic. I'm sure if Tom were to read this, he would say "Hey, you gotta do what you gotta do" and shake it off like it was nothing. But I know different. And I know I've found the love of my life all over again. I know he loves me for me and that's what I've always wanted in my life. (Hey, anyone who tells me I'm beautiful when I'm bald is a keeper in my book!)*

January 24, 2002

1. Tests that aren't scheduled until the afternoon
2. Semi-good hospital food
3. Prayers from strangers
4. Nurses who are quite during the night
5. Visitors tomorrow

January 25, 2002

1. Familiar faces
2. Feeling good
3. Laughing with Stacie
4. Getting a pool table
5. All of my tests coming back good.

Well, I'm still in the hospital and I'm starting to get really bored. I'm so tired of setting in this bed and watching the same TV shows. I have to go to the bathroom every 50 minutes. It gets really pesky. I watched a show on Oprah this afternoon about finding out who you are and your mission in life. They made it seem so simple – I'm still confused. I guess I'll just have to let life lead me there.

January 26, 2002

1. Phone calls from home
2. Getting moved into our new house
3. Seeing Tom tomorrow
4. Conversations with strangers
5. 3 more treatments left

Day 5 of my next to last MTX treatment. I've started the bitter feeling and being mad about being here. I got to talk to a mother of a 10-year-old leukemia patient who is on his 2nd relapse. He was diagnosed when he was 2 years old. This is the only life Nathan has ever known. He comes from a normal family and life. You just never know about how life will turn with you. It just keeps turning.

Tom got us moved into the house today. Poor Sam has no clue what's going on. Tom told me that he'll be up tomorrow – I can't wait. My level is .20 so I think I'll drink a few cups of water before I go to sleep. tI might help – who knows. My mind is too busy to sleep anyway.

I've met so many wonderful people while I've been up here. My life is better for having met these people. I guess there's a silver lining for just about everything. It's all about finding it.

My mind is racing like crazy. I feel like screaming, but I don't have a specific reason for it. I feel so lonely, but I've been talking to people all night. I'm so unsettled in my life, it seems like I shouldn't be planning or even think about the future. But the future is all I have to hold on to. I sit here and think about the past and what I used to want. I wanted to know I was special and that people cared for me – check. I wanted to always believe that Tom was absolutely the "one for me – check. Build a life and home with him – check (half). Have a family – still open. Be a success – what? In what way – how do you measure that? I guess that has changed for me. Right now, a success for me means being happy. I feel I have been successful in chemo because I've never backed down from it. I've been scared, but I've never let it beat me. I can't imagine being a kid and having courage to face it. I guess I'm allowed to be proud of myself for getting this far. Some times the hardest person to give credit to is yourself. There's always a feeling or thought that you should have done something different – better. You never see what you've accomplished. I guess when this is all over, I'll have to remember to give myself a pat on the back.

We Have A House…

January 27, 2002

1. Visits from Tom
2. Taco salads from Wendy's
3. Getting doctors on your side
4. Relaxing music
5. The idea that I have a house

Well, here I still sit at Children's. I've done all I was told, but my MTX level is still at .16 (needs to be lover than .10). I've become so frustrated with the system of this specific chemo. I give up.

I'm so excited to get to the house and see it. I'm really anxious to start making it a home. Tom says that Sam is still really scared. I can't wait to get home so maybe I can comfort her a little. I really do feel like a mother, worrying about her all of the time.

Tom was up today. Josh, Steph, Scooter, Matt P., and Jeff were at the house last night. Tom is pretty tired. Hopefully he can start relaxing a little more, now that we're actually in the house. I just hope everyone gives us some space now. We need some time to relax and "get away" from everyone. Not that I don't want people to visit or call, I would just like for it to be on our terms now. I guess we'll see how it goes.

A lot of times, when I've started to write in this journal, I haven't had a clue about what I was going to write about. My feelings and thoughts just seemed to flow out pretty easily. I've realized some pretty important things, too. I don't want to waste this incredible gift I have been given. I guess this will give me incentive to do it right then, right?

1/28/02

Ginger was released in the evening at 6:00pm – her counts were .09.

2/5/02

Ginger went back to Columbus with a fever of 100.2 degrees. Her cat Samantha has a fever of 103 degrees and was given antibiotics at the vet yesterday.

2/6/02

Roger did well at therapy, he gained several degrees on the machine. Ginger is meeting a new girl that was diagnosed with cancer tomorrow, she hopes to help her by talking with her.

2/7/02

We're hoping Ginger gets home for my birthday, but she still had a fever this am of 102 degrees. She came home!

2/11/02

Ginger had blood drawn at MMH and her ANC was 6,000, but her platelets were only 23, they have to be at least 50 before she can have chemo again, so she won't have her treatment tomorrow as scheduled.

2/13/02

Ginger had blood drawn again at MMH.

2/14/02

Valentines Day!! Ginger was admitted for chemo, she'll be there about six days, next to last treatment.

2/16/02

Ginger has blisters on her feet and all of her fingers from her chemo.

The Last Treatment Admittance...

February 15, 2002

1. *Visits from friends*
2. *Sam feeling better*
3. *Getting the house in order*
4. *Last chemo admittance*
5. *Getting a pool table*

Well, here I sit – room 5314 for my last methotrexate. I still can't believe it's almost over. Next week, I'll have my last treatment, then a fever after that. Then we start to climb back towards a normal life.

Tom and Scooter came up to visit today. Tom is coming back up tomorrow to spend the night tomorrow night. I was setting on the bed this afternoon with Tom watching Aladdin and he reached over and touched my shoulder. I realized just how much I miss this touch. I see how much a hug from him means to me. We've really been careful during treatments not to get too close, I guess for fear of germs. Kind of like when you're kids and you don't want to touch a boy because he probably has kooties. We used to touch a lot – just small things like holding hands that you don't notice at the time, but miss when it's gone. In bed we used to hold each other and since my surgery, that's stopped too. I don't blame Tom or myself for this – we've just given each other space. I just miss it – a lot.

I've also thought a lot about friendship – and how great it's been to see how strong Tom & I's relationship is. It's very safe to say our relationship has not been physical for the past 7 months. We've also built a home in that time – a feat that usually sets people against each other. I have got so much support from Tom, so much love & pampering. I don't even know if Tom realizes how much he has given me in a time that it was hard for me to ask for help. And that is what I have learned about friendship – friends can see when you need help and support and they give you what you need without you having to ask. They just know by instinct and an intimate knowledge of your mind and thoughts.

I see a lot of things I have to learn to accept. Well, I guess there's some things I have to wait to get back and two things I must accept. I have to wait for my hair to grow back – a feat that can't happen fast enough for me. I have to wait for (& work at) strength in my knee to return. I have to have patience for my swelling to go down and to gain confidence and balance in my leg again. I have to accept my 2 scars – leg & chest. I don't know that it's I need to accept it, actually I think it's getting used to them. Any time I start to feel self-conscience of my scars, I'll just bring to mind what they represent and mean – my life. It's very easy to say that my life is so much more important than cosmetic things.

I hope that when life gets back to a normal schedule and a normal life again, I remember how precious life is. When I'm depressed about not being able to do some of the things I could do bc. I hope I remember I'm lucky to be alive. I hope I don't ever think I deserve special treatment for my situation. I never want to think that I deserve special treatment, I never should just be given special treatment just because. At the same time, I hope people want to know and learn about my experiences. I want them to ask questions and become more aware of certain things in life.

My life will never be the same, but in some ways, it will be better. I have always tried not to take life for granted, but never had things put into perspective so clearly. Day-to-day life is so precious, more so than I had ever imagined. Being able to go to the store without checking on my counts before I feel safe in doing so, it will be wonderful.

Being able to make love to Tom – to kiss him, to hold him and feel beautiful for him – these are the things I am looking forward to the most.

2/19/02
I went to Columbus and got Ginger – her level was .09. Roger went to see his diabetes doctor at 4:45, he is looking for sleep apnia, depression or low thyroid.

2/20/02
Roger had blood drawn at his doctor's office. We should get the results in a week. Ginger had labs done at MMH. Her levels were fine for chemo.

2/21/02

Ginger has doxo chemo.

2/22/02
Ginger's last chemo treatment, she drove to Columbus and Linda Sue rode with her. She came back to Opal's because Tom was afraid he was getting the flu. Roger got his test results back and his thyroid is low. He has further tests on 2/27&28 at MMH.

2/27/02
Justin's 24th birthday. Ginger went to Columbus for tests.

2/28/02
Ginger had to have blood in Columbus. Opal took her up, she had 3 units they got home at 6:30 and she had a fever of 100.5 at 8:00pm. So Tom took off work and they went back to Columbus.

3/3/02
Ginger came home from hopefully her last fever at 1:30pm.

3/8/02
Ginger had to be in Columbus for the removal of her port at 12:00, her surgery is scheduled for 1:30. Roger, Tom, Mike (Boog), Opal, mom and I all joined Ginger for surgery. We left Columbus at 4:00. Aunt Debbie was killed in an auto accident last night.

3/11/02

Roger went to Morgantown to see his surgeon and the visit went well. He goes back on May 13th. He has 116 degrees of bend. Ginger's leg gave out on her in Wal-Mart parking lot & she fell.

3/14/02

Ginger saw Dr. W., had x-rays done and she doesn't have to go back for 6 months. He wrote her a prescription for therapy 3xweek for 2 months.

Back to "Normal"...

3/17/02

1. *Being done with treatments*
2. *Getting the house organized*
3. *Playing with Sam*
4. *Having friends over to our house*
5. *Finding some clothes that fit*

It's pretty late right now, but I wanted to write again. Tomorrow, I start back to work. I'm only working ½ days for now so that I don't wear myself out. I'm sort of nervous – lots of new things and people. It will take awhile to get back into the swing of things.

I'm feeling really good – a lot better than during chemo. I'm starting to get some peach fuzz on my head. I've gained 25 lbs. So I'm getting clothes from Carol and Linda S. I can't wait until I lose this weight so I can wear my own clothes. I hope to start physical therapy this week.

It's late and I need to get to bed – I've got a big day tomorrow. Kind of like another first day of work. I'll write more later.

3/18/02

1. *Being back at work*
2. *Seeing old friends*
3. *Feeling stronger every day*
4. *Loving Tom*
5. *A nap in the afternoon*

6. *Balloons and cake from my co-workers*

Well, I'm a working woman again! I worked 8-12 am. There's a lot of new stuff to get used to again. New office, roomie, telephone, desk, co-workers, schedule, etc. It feels strange being back there – it actually feels all wrong. I'm not comfortable at all. I don't know what it is exactly – maybe that it's all new. Kelly is not there to talk to anymore – I have to walk and stand around if I want to talk to her. It might take a while to connect with Lori. I feel like I don't know how to talk to anyone at work. I don't feel like I have anything in common with them anymore. I'm not the same person I was bc. It's like I can't take anything there seriously. Over the past 9 months, I have trained myself not to look at the petty things in this world – it seems like that's all they look at down there. I don't know how to deal with this, not yet. I guess I'll have to give it time.

I start therapy on my knee on Wednesday. I'm pretty excited about it. And I'm a little nervous, too. I hope to do so well but what if I don't? It's been easy up to this point.

Everyone at work liked my wig. They say it looks so natural. It still looks fake to me, but what else do I expect?

I'm having a hard time finding myself. I don't know the person I want to be. It's really hard to go from chemo patient to real world person. I can't focus on "real world" things and I can't get things in priority. This part is going to be hard – and it's the part I was looking forward to. Hopefully, this will pass quickly.

The life of a cancer patient changes drastically when treatment ends and "normal" life begins. I didn't have someone looking over me each day, no one to tell my little pains to. I was so used to asking Stacy if such & such was normal, it was hard to adjust to doctoring myself. Then I wasn't sure what I could diagnose on my own – should I call her and see what's going on? I'm sure there were times that Stacy would just roll her eyes on the other end of the phone and say, "No, Ginger. That's fine." Such a patient angel.

My first trip to Children's as a cancer survivor was strange. I didn't have to go through admissions, didn't have to carry an armload of bags and suit cases for a six-day stay. I got to sign in like I was at any other doctor's office. I actually had to sit and wait in a waiting room – unlike when I was taken to the ER with one of my 103-degree fevers, I was rushed to my own room – no waiting allowed.

Height, weight – those were normal. Get blood taken – ahh, I recognize this. Questions about how I was feeling, right down to the most minute detail – yes, I am back at home. I was surrounded by things that were normal for me, from that patient world. It was a comfort because I knew what to expect from these things, I had built my daily routine around them.

Then came the nervous parts – tests. The x-rays, bone scans, and audio tests that show how you're really doing. I had felt a knot in my stomach for a full week before returning to Columbus. What if it came back? What would I do? Would something be wrong with my metal knee? What if I have to take more medicine? Every person in my family had drilled me before I left, "You are going to call me, right?" I replied that I would, but in my mind I was thinking "only if it's good news."

I couldn't think of anything else until I heard the results of those first month's tests – all clear. No one could have realized what kind of stress I was under until I heard those words from Stacy. Tears of joy flowed as my emotions let loose. I had won the first of many rounds. I slept soundly that night.

The stress level before each following check-up lessened as my confidence grew. I eventually let my mind wonder to other things besides my leg and my next check-up. I grew accustomed to looking at life, instead of worrying at losing it.

I could see that my family was slowly doing the same thing. I remember hearing the relief in my dad's voice when we got the good news after my first check-up. During treatments, I had realized that everyone who cared for me was going through their own type of chemo – it affected everyone. Each time we received good news from tests, it was another victory for them, too.

In A Perfect World...

I was asked by Julie of the Washington County American Cancer Society to write an article for the Relay for Life newsletter. Little did I know, this article would provide me with a speech that would make me a requested speaker in the years to follow. I have titled it "In a Perfect World" and I believe that it fits the article perfectly.

"In a perfect world....
By Ginger McConnell

In a perfect world, no one would develop cancer – it simply wouldn't exist. No one would be sick or lose their hair, everyone would feel strong, nobody would need to worry, and no one would lose their battle with the disease. Sounds like a nice place, doesn't it? Unfortunately, this isn't a perfect world, and people of all ages and races are diagnosed with cancer every day. They will face the unknown world of cancer. And I know the fear they are facing all too well, because I have stood in their shoes.

At the age of 23, I developed a pain and swelling in my left knee. It hurt to do ordinary things, like walking or going up steps. After several x-rays and tests, it was determined that I had a tumor at the end of my femur. A trip to a specialist in Columbus confirmed that I had a rare type of bone cancer – osteogenic sarcoma.

In an instant, there I stood, facing that unknown world. It didn't seem possible – just 10 months before, I was enjoying my fairy tale wedding. Only 5 days before, my husband and I were signing the loan papers to build our new home. I was just settling into my new job, and life was getting to a state of normal. Besides, I was only 23 years old – I was too young to have cancer.

I was truly blessed when I was referred to Children's Hospital in Columbus, Ohio for my treatment. The minute my family and I stepped into the facility, I was treated like I was the most important person there. It didn't seem to matter to the staff that I was 23 years old – five years over the age limit of patients normally accepted at Children's. They explained to me what was going to happen with my treatment and the side effects that I could experience.

I had gone into this thinking that I was too young to have cancer. Sitting in the waiting room of the Hematology Clinic, I saw first hand what "too young to have cancer" meant. There were children with tubes hooked up to them, smiling and playing. There were children who didn't have hair, and it didn't bother them. What struck me was that they didn't know that this wasn't a normal life – they had never known anything different than this hospital. These children would prove to be an enormous source of inspiration, strength, and hope to me during my long, and sometimes, unforgiving battle.

I went through 10 months of chemotherapy and a full knee replacement to get rid of the cancer. It was a long struggle – I developed fevers many times during treatment, which added to my time in the hospital. There were many days when I didn't feel like moving, let alone having a normal life. Losing my hair was one of the hardest things I had to deal with. Everyone tried to convince me that I was beautiful even without hair, but that was as hard to swallow as the handful of pills I had to take on a daily basis. There were many times that I cried myself to sleep, but there was *something* that would not let me give up. And all of the hard times and troubles were worth it – I am currently a *10 month cancer survivor.*

My first Relay was just a few months after I had finished with my treatments in 2002. I really didn't know what to expect when I got there. I was directed towards the survivor tent to sign up. I couldn't believe all of the wonderful gifts they had for me! The bag of goodies that I received was great, and I felt so special to wear the Hawaiian lei around my neck to show that I was a survivor. It warmed my heart to see the number of people that were wearing them, too!! They were normal, every day people, just like me!!

If this special attention had stopped with the bag of goodies, I would have been perfectly content. It didn't. The group of survivors helped to kick off the event by walking the first lap, and let me tell you, this is an experience that I will never forget. I was overwhelmed with emotion as I walked around that park with the other survivors. Everyone crowded around the path and clapped their hands and cheered for us as we took our lap. I couldn't stop myself from crying. These people were congratulating me for my victory over cancer. It was this lap that showed me that this event was much more than a fundraiser for the battle against cancer. It was also a celebration for the people who have already won their battle.

It was a cold and rainy night, but that didn't dampen the spirits of the crowd. The celebration continued, and the teams had fun participating in the various events during the night. I was getting pretty tired, and my knee was starting to hurt in the cold, damp weather. I was ready to go home, when a friend encouraged me to stay for the Luminary service. "It's beautiful," she said, so I decided to stay to see what it was all about. I am so glad I stayed. I was helping with the luminaries that our team had, when I started to read the names that were on the bags. I found one that read "Ginger McConnell" – wow, what a great feeling to know that someone had thought to honor me at this ceremony. After a few more bags were handed to me, another name made me freeze. The bag read "Kandis Kay Moore." It was a bag for my mother, who had died of cancer when I was only four years old. It was at that very moment that I discovered another aspect of the event – the honoring of those who had lost their battle. My mom didn't know that she had cancer and wasn't able to fight the disease, but I had been given the opportunity to fight and win my battle. I placed the two bags next to each other, and while I stood there looking at them, I started to cry. My mom would have been proud of my fight, and I knew it. A stranger walked by and saw me crying, "It's okay," she said and hugged me. Somehow, I knew that this stranger understood what I was going through.

I look back on my first Relay with fond memories. This event helps raise money for cancer research, celebrates the victory of survivors, and honors those who have lost their battle. It really recognizes the past, present, and future of those with cancer. We can see how far we have come and that we are not alone. Even in a world that is less than perfect, we are striving to make it that way."

Life After Cancer...

I was surprised that life was not perfect the minute that I stopped treatment. I had this illusion in my mind that life would be perfect and I would be back to normal a week after treatments ended. Instead, I faced being tired and not feeling "like myself" like I had imagined. I had looked forward to going to Wal-Mart and shopping by myself. I soon found out that I needed to park close to the door and know exactly where I was going in the store because I was just not strong enough to do it yet. I also expected to be able to go back to work as usual. I ended up working half days for two weeks and went home exhausted every afternoon. It was so hard for me to accept that life was not going to be sunny skies right off the bat.

I consider myself a strong person, and the letdown of my physical limitations took their toll. On the outside, I focused all of my strength to make it appear that I was getting along great. It was easy at first because everyone was so supportive of me and always told me how proud they were of me for the battle that I had won. No one, not even Tom, knew that I was so sad inside, and that this outer appearance of happiness and strength was just a mask. How could I tell them that I wasn't happy? I had beat cancer, and I had so many things in my life that were absolutely wonderful. How could I be unhappy with that? So many people would be lucky to have the things and the people that I have in my life. I started to tell myself that the feeling would go away, and I didn't tell anyone because I thought that they would think I was just being selfish and spoiled. I mean really, what else could I want out of life?

Not telling those who were close to me about the feelings that I was having was the worst decision of my life. Yes, I was a strong person, but I was a strong person that needed help. But I wasn't willing to ask for it because everyone had already given so much of themselves to me already. They had lives of their own to live. This was my problem to deal with.

Tom & I had so many plans for the future. During treatment, we would talk about them, and those dreams would get me through a bad day. I would think, "In 15 years I'll be sitting on the porch of our home and this will just be a memory," or "I'll be holding our baby in my arms and all of this pain will have been worth it." But as time went on, those dreams didn't seem like my own anymore. I didn't want to work for a home of our own, and I certainly didn't want a child. But Tom held onto these dreams, and would talk about them often.

One day he asked me, "So when do you want to have our first kid?" The question hit me like a brick. How do I tell him never?

He went on, "I can tell you what I want for Christmas next year – a little blue eyed, blonde haired girl. What do you think of that?" I guess I had been thinking of a shirt and a CD. Not exactly what he had in mind.

"Tom," I said, "I'm just not ready to have kids yet. I have spent the last 10 months of my life in a hospital with doctors poking and prodding me, I want some time to myself."

This was the truth; I did want time to myself. And, I deserved the break. The further away from a hospital I got, the happier I was. I just didn't tell him that, at that time, I had no interest in children. That would have crushed him. I also didn't mention that the house plans were on hold. One more thing was bothering me – him.

It took me a while to recognize what was going on. There are times in a marriage when couples get tired of each other, and I had gone into this marriage fully expecting these times. In the beginning, I told myself that this was just one of those stages, and that it would eventually pass. But then I started to get more annoyed with Tom, and I can see now for no reason. I didn't want to hold his hand, or kiss him. Sex was definitely out of the question. I began to question my feelings for him – something that I had a really hard time with. I just didn't understand what was going on with our relationship. If I wasn't physically attracted to my husband, what did that say about how I felt about him?

Tom and I had always had a very open relationship. I finally decided that I would talk to him about some of what I had been feeling. I explained to him that I just wasn't happy with my life anymore. I was no longer interested in the things that used to make me happy. I said that I just didn't know what was going on, and that I didn't know what to do to fix how I felt. Then he hit me with the question that I knew was coming,

"What about us? Are we okay?"

I had to be honest in my answer; it's not in my nature to lie, and especially not to Tom.

"Tom, right now I don't know. You are my best friend, and I can't imagine my life without you. I just don't know what's going on right now."

"Ginger, I don't want to be just your best friend, I want to be your husband."

He asked what he could do to help and I told him that I couldn't tell him one thing that he could do to fix it. I didn't have one complaint about him -- he had always been wonderful. And, he continued to be wonderful.

"I think you should talk to Stacy about what you're feeling."

It made perfect sense. Stacy would understand what was going on. She would be able to help. That night, I lay in Tom's arm, and was at peace with what we had discussed. I would talk to Stacy and see what she said.

An email to Stacy about what I was feeling sparked an emotional response from her. She said that it sounded like I was suffering from depression, and that this type of thing was not unusual among people who have went through a life-changing event like I had. She urged me to see a psychologist, and offered to help me find one. One thing that Stacy told me was that I had taken an important step in understanding what was going on and taking the initiative to do something about it. This is usually the hardest part for people to go through.

Yes, it was hard to admit that I was suffering from depression, but it was just as hard to fix it. I went to a psychologist for a while, but I wasn't telling her anything that I hadn't already talked to Tom about. She tried to turn it into a marriage problem, but I knew that that wasn't the problem because there wasn't anything that I could tell her that Tom was doing wrong, or that I felt he could do to fix it. If it were something as simple as that, then Tom and I would have dealt with that on our own.

I also tried a depression drug, after talking to another psychologist at Children's, who finally did confirm my suspicion, and diagnosed me with depression. The drugs make me feel better mentally, but ended up putting more a strain on Tom and I because of the sexual side effects.

As time went by, Tom and I had a lot of stressful moments, and had another discussion like the one mentioned previously. But through it all, Tom never gave up on me. There were many times that I thought in my head that I wasn't sure that I was still in love with him – I loved him, but I wasn't sure that I was IN love with him. But every time I had the feeling that I wasn't sure, my heart made me realize just that – I wasn't sure. I wasn't sure that if I did separate from Tom that that would make me happy. At one point, he flat out asked me, "Do you want a divorce?" I couldn't say yes – I couldn't imagine my life without him in it. I replied that I didn't, and his reply was "Okay, then we'll be alright."

The turning point in my depression, and the confusing feelings in my head about my heart and Tom, was a trip that Tom and I took in the fall of 2003. Tom woke up early one Sunday morning and, after a lot of persuading to get me out of bed, we drove to Old Man's Cave – a place that we had went while we were dating.

Tom and I love the outdoors, and this was a perfect time to take this trip. The leaves were starting to turn to their fall colors, and the drive was beautiful. We took trails that I could walk easily with my knee, and enjoyed the beautiful nature around us. We hiked back to see beautiful waterfalls, and rock formations. Eventually, I got brave and wondered off the trail to more challenging trails. I took my camera and practiced my photography skills. We ate at a local steakhouse, and drove home after spending an entire day away, together with nature.

This trip brought me back to what I loved about life, and Tom. I knew that I had chosen the right path in life, and, although it wouldn't always be perfect, I was going to be okay. Tom and I were going to be okay. I guess Tom always knew that, he was just waiting on me to see that. It was strange that it took something as simple as a day trip to bring things into perspective – but I know that there was a higher power working that day.

I found another love for the second time in the summer of 2003 – softball. I had always been told that I would never be able to play softball again because of my knee replacement. The added movement and jarring would lessen the life of the replacement, and mean another surgery sooner than expected. I had coached my high school softball team that year, but I wasn't satisfied standing on the sidelines. A trip to my orthopedic surgeon proved to be one of the best days of my life.

The doctor told me that I could play softball as long as I played first base and had someone run the bases for me when I hit. I made him repeat himself a few times before I would actually believe that he had said it – voluntarily. I know that when I walked out of that office, I had a smile on my face so big, everyone in that office knew that I had just gotten good news.

The perfect setting for my return to softball – playing in the fire department softball tournament with the Sheriff's Department team. What could be better than that? I was so excited to be on the field with those guys. I was ready to play first base, and I had been collecting the courage to do the one that that I wasn't supposed to do – run. I wasn't going to go completely crazy; I was just going to run to first base, and then get a runner for the rest. This weekend meant so much to me – I was really excited to be able to play again. My poor office-mate had to hear me talk about it the entire week before.

Well, it rained that weekend – a lot. That made the field extremely muddy. The muddy conditions didn't lend well to my plans of running – it was risky enough to do on a field in good condition, but the mud made it too risky. While I would still play first base with the team, I would get someone else to bat for me. While the fact that I wasn't batting made me sad, the weekend was wonderful anyway. The first throw to me was the first test – I had to dig it out of the dirt: and I did. It was so natural for me to be out there. Now, I will say that I had to make some adjustments, and there were a few times that I stepped the wrong way and felt a twinge of pain. But the pain was minimal to the elation that I felt during that entire tournament. The Sheriff's Department won the tournament – a perfect ending to a perfect comeback.

As sweet as that weekend was, there was still something that I was missing. But, I got the change to complete my softball return in the fall. I was asked to play on a co-ed fall league – I explained that I had to play first base and needed a runner after I got to first base, and they agreed to my conditions– they would love to have me on their team.

I had practiced running in my living room to prepare for my softball debut. I put on my brace and practice jogging a few steps at first. I needed to see how it was going to feel to start out of the batter's box. I was expecting pain to shoot up my leg as soon as I took my first stride – but, instead nothing. Not a single pain. It was amazing; and wonderful. Eventually I got brave and took a few more strides. I can't say that it was pretty, but I was running. I was really looking forward to my first game back.

Well, here it was – opening night. I was so excited, and so nervous. It felt so good for me to be playing again. The first time I stepped up to the plate, my heart was beating hard enough that I could hear it in my ear. I had practiced running in the parking lot before the game, but I wasn't sure what the outcome would be. On the first pitch, I broke my own rule of not swinging on the first pitch, and swung. It wasn't the best pitch, and the result was a little grounder to third base. As I started to run to first base after contact, instinct took over in my head. I froze in the batter's box. And just like that, I was the third out of the inning, and I was left standing there, looking like an idiot.

I could see that the members on my team that didn't know my story were confused, but no one on said anything to me about not running. I was so mad at myself – if this is what was going to happen the rest of the season, I was going to quit the team. I walked back to the dugout and grabbed my glove. As I walked to my position, I was yelling at myself in my mind – I looked like an idiot. This was the night that I was supposed to shine, and instead, I hadn't.

But, I had another turn at the plate, and this time, I didn't disappoint myself. I hit the ball far enough into the outfield that I didn't have to worry about running fast – but I ran. It wasn't pretty, but I ran. I stood on first base and waived to my teammates for a runner to replace me. Outside, I'm sure I looked like someone who was glad to get a hit, but on the inside, I was yelling with excitement. This was the moment that I had taken my life back – my entire life. Cancer had taken many things from my life, and I had managed to get most of them back. Softball was the last thing that it had, and this was the moment that I had taken it back. It was my life again, and I could now say that I was triumphant. It felt really good.

As the season went on, my running improved – and so did my hitting. I got to play with one of my friends, Chris that played on the Sheriff's team. It was a lot of fun to be his teammate instead of the lady that kept the stats. Chris had stayed after many games with a few of my friends to pitch to me so that I could get ready to play again. It meant a lot to me to play with a friend. It meant a lot to play.

That was the only season that I actually played softball. I did improve over the course of the season, but I never played to the caliber that I did before my surgery. Although playing that summer did more for me than I could ever explain, it just wasn't the same for me. I continued to coach my high school team, and keep book for the Sheriff's department team so I could stay involved in the game, but I've never really played on a team since that summer.

Now that our life was calming down and returning to a somewhat normal life together, Tom and I had discussed the idea of having children; but I had my reservations. I have just spent the last 12 months of my life in a hospital, being poked and prodded, and never getting a moment to myself. I really just wanted a few years for the two of us. We put it in the back of our minds, but the thought was always there.

Finally, in the winter of 2003, I told Tom that I was ready to start trying. I had some conditions though – I didn't want this to consume our lives. I didn't want to have to take my temperature every day and gauge when the best time would be. I didn't want this to control our lives. And, if things didn't work out and I couldn't get pregnant, then we both agreed that we would adopt – there are so many children in this world that need love, and we were sure that we had enough to give.

Just to be sure that things were okay to even try, we scheduled an appointment with specialists in Columbus. February of that year, we sat in a doctor's office and heard, "it's perfectly okay to try – all should be alright. We'll see you in a few months."

When we got in the car, we both laughed at the doctor's optimism – a few months, yeah, right.

A few months later, the varsity softball team was playing in a tournament, and I had taken the afternoon off to travel with them. I wanted to get as much exposure to coaching as I could. I was a few days late, but hadn't mentioned that to Tom. I still had a funny feeling about it, though. Could I be pregnant? No way, I was feeling fine, and we really hadn't been trying. Still, I had this feeling…

I had gotten off work around noon, but didn't need to be at the high school until 2:00 to leave. So, I decided to go to the grocery store and get a test. I felt weird, but I made it through the checkout and home without bugging out too much.

That was, until I saw that the test was positive. I froze – wow. Then I thought – now what? I was home alone, and I wasn't going to see Tom until later that night when I got back from the softball game. I couldn't call my mom because I wanted to talk to Tom first. And, this wasn't something that I wanted to tell someone over the phone.

I was shaking and I needed to tell someone, I guess to make it real for me. I went out to my Aunt Linda's – it seemed appropriate that the first person I had talked to about my cancer was the first person that I told I was going to have a baby.

Trying to act normal, I followed her around as she picked up toys. Finally, I just said it – "Aunt Linda, I'm pregnant."

I wasn't sure how she would react – gosh, I guess I wasn't sure how I was going to react. Smile, tears, congratulations – all of that and more. I swore her to secrecy as I left, being sure that she knew that Tom hadn't been informed yet.

I went to the game, but it was a blur. I wanted to tell everyone, but I didn't dare tell anyone else before I told Tom. We lost the game, which made the ride home longer. We stopped to eat, but I couldn't find much of an appetite. I was trying to figure out how I was going to tell Tom that he was going to be a dad.

When I got home, my stomach was in knots. Tom was sitting on the couch, and was getting ready to make him a sandwich. I started doing busy work around the kitchen, telling him about the boring details of the game, and my day. We passed each other in the kitchen a few times, and finally I stopped and watched him making his sandwich.

"Well, I have a question for you." I at least got his attention.

"How do you feel about being called "Dad"?"

It was Christmas Eve and the doctor broke my water at 9:30 that morning. After 45 minutes of actual labor, our little miracle, Levi Dean McConnell, was born a healthy baby at 4:15 pm. He was three weeks early, but his lungs were well developed, and he was proving it. Tom was inspecting him at the warmer, informing me from across the room that he had his fingers. Out of all of the holidays that I had spent in the hospital, this was the best. And, it made those other holidays worth it.

I wish that I had a camera in my eyes to capture all of the love and joy that I see in Levi every day. I wish that I could say that I never worried about the cancer coming back, but his smile and laughter makes it easier to put those thoughts in the back of my mind.

Final Thoughts...

You know, during my whole ordeal, I never once thought that cancer would change the person that I was. I felt that I was a pretty good person, why change? I like me. Boy, was I naive.

Looking back on me before, during, and after cancer, I can see a different person. Sure, there are the physical things like my hair being shorter and my scar, but there were definitely three different people during those time periods. Before cancer, I wanted to please everyone. I wanted to make sure that people liked me. During cancer, I seemed to fade away from what people thought – not because I didn't care anymore, I just wasn't up to worrying about it. Now, I see that I would like it if people liked me, but if they don't like me for who I am, their friendship isn't really friendship at all. I don't have time in my life to worry about the insignificant things. If small things end a friendship or a relationship, then it wasn't much of one to begin with. People don't normally have that perspective – they are worrying about making others happy with the small things. And, I have another little person to care for now.

But it's the little things that are wonderful – that kiss on the cheek from your husband, just because; a smile from your son that came from nowhere; a phone call from a friend who just wanted to say hello. It was those little things that got me through my sickness.

I remember taking my first step after my knee replacement. I only walked from my bed to the door of my room and back, but the joy that those few steps brought me was out of this world. I remember the floors perfectly – wood with a lot of scratches in it. I can even remember thinking that that day was one of the most important days of my life. My surgery was a turning point in my treatment. It signified the time that cancer was no longer part of my body and that I was winning. I knew that there was a long, tough road ahead of me, but news that the tumor was 85-90% dead when removed fueled me that much more. I remember it was in those first steps that I told myself that I was going to be okay. Just think how many steps that you take in a day. You probably don't give it one thought. I took a dozen, and those little steps had a huge impact on my life.

Take the time to look at the little steps – those steps are leading you on your journey in life: make them good ones.

www.ingramcontent.com/pod-product-compliance
Lightning Source LLC
LaVergne TN
LVHW011421080426
835512LV00005B/192